Series / Number 07-048

# MODELS FOR INNOVATION DIFFUSION

**VIJAY MAHAJAN**
*Southern Methodist University*

**ROBERT A. PETERSON**
*University of Texas at Austin*

**SAGE** PUBLICATIONS
*The International Professional Publishers*
Newbury Park   London   New Delhi

*11-8-95*

*For information address:*

SAGE Publications, Inc.
2455 Teller Road
Newbury Park, California 91320

SAGE Publications Ltd.
6 Bonhill Street
London EC2A 4PU
United Kingdom

SAGE Publications India Pvt. Ltd.
M-32 Market
Greater Kailash I
New Delhi 110 048 India

International Standard Book Number 0-8039-2136-5

Library of Congress Catalog Card No. 85-050011

94  10  9  8  7  6  5

---

When citing a professional paper, please use the proper form. Remember to cite the
correct Sage University Paper series title and include the paper number. One of the
following formats can be adapted (depending on the style manual used):

(1) IVERSEN, GUDMUND R. and NORPOTH, HELMUT (1976) "Analysis of
Variance." Sage University Paper series on Quantitative Applications in the Social
Sciences, 07-001. Beverly Hills and London: Sage Pubns.

*OR*

(2) Iversen, Gudmund R. and Norpoth, Helmut. 1976. *Analysis of Variance.* Sage
University Paper series on Quantitative Applications in the Social Sciences, series no.
07-001. Beverly Hills and London: Sage Pubns.

# CONTENTS

## Series Editor's Introduction

As the authors note in their introduction, the diffusion process is one of the most widely studied of social processes, with research now found in virtually all of the social sciences, in education, in geography, and in numerous business applications. The topics studied vary from such widely-used phenomena as credit cards to such specialized topics as the spread of basic oxygen furnaces among steel manufacturers.

Such widespread interest results in a lively intellectual environment and frequent new findings, but it also has some potential disadvantages. For one thing, the same theoretical discoveries and similar empirical results tend to be rediscovered in each discipline. Second, it means that students and researchers interested in the topic must be conversant with the notation and language of several disciplines if they are to be familiar with the best and most recent work.

The vast amount of work on diffusion and its setting in such a variety of disciplines simply beg for an introduction that bridges intellectual domains and sets out basic findings in a clear and consistent way. *Models for Innovation Diffusion*, by Vijay Mahajan and Robert A. Peterson meets this need. They present a lucid, state-of-the-art introduction to the powerful tools for investigating the temporal diffusion process of any innovation. Although their approach is abstract and general, they consistently try to be integrative by making frequent references to work from numerous areas. They also make their work more approachable by the inclusion of a number of helpful examples.

In Chapter 2, Mahajan and Peterson present a "fundamental" deterministic diffusion model that permits them to review and integrate several widely cited diffusion models. In addition to covering issues related to the estimation and interpretation of model parameters, this section emphasizes both explicit and implicit assumptions underlying the employment of the fundamental diffusion model. Chapter 3 consists of a discussion of "flexible" diffusion models. These models are pattern-sensitive and can accommodate a variety of diffusion patterns.

5

Chapter 4 contains selected advanced diffusion models including dynamic models, multi-innovation models, space and time models, and models that directly incorporate influencing or change agents. Chapter 5 contains applications of diffusion models in a variety of contexts and should convey to the reader the generality of the models across disciplines and innovations. Chapter 6 concludes with technical suggestions for further development and use of diffusion models.

Our monographs are designed to appeal to readers throughout the social sciences. More than ever, this is true of the present volume and we are pleased to add it to our list.

—*Richard G. Niemi*
Series Co-Editor

# MODELS FOR INNOVATION DIFFUSION

**VIJAY MAHAJAN**
*Southern Methodist University*

**ROBERT A. PETERSON**
*University of Texas at Austin*

## 1. BASIC CONCEPTS

**The diffusion** of an innovation has traditionally been defined as the process by which that innovation "is communicated through certain channels over time among the members of a social system" (Rogers, 1983: 5). As such, there are four key elements in the diffusion process: the *innovation, channels of communication, time,* and the *social system.* An innovation is any idea, object, or practice that is perceived as new by members of the social system and can range from a rumor to a rocket ship, a surfboard to a supermarket scanning system. Communication channels are the means by which information is transmitted to or within the social system. Mass media communication channels include radio, television, newspapers, and magazines. Interpersonal communication channels are the face-to-face linkages between two or more members of the social system. Time relates to the rate at which the innovation is diffused or the relative speed with which it is adopted by members of the social system. In the present context, the social system consists of individuals, organizations, or agencies that share a common "culture" and are potential adopters of the innovation. Hence, members of a social system can range from students enrolled in a specific course or consumers living in a particular neighborhood, to business organizations and governmental agencies, to states and nations.

Research on the diffusion of innovations has resulted in a body of literature consisting of several thousand articles, books, and assorted publications. Indeed, the diffusion process is perhaps one of the most widely researched and best documented social phenomena. To date, research on the diffusion process has been reported in nearly two dozen

7

**TABLE 1.1**
**Illustrative Diffusion Pattern Investigations**

| Investigator | Innovation | Social System |
|---|---|---|
| Rapoport (1978) | Radioisotopes | U.S. hospitals |
| Perry and Kraemer (1978) | Computer applications | Local governments |
| Malecki (1977) | Credit card | Ohio banks |
| Brown and Philliber (1977) | Planned parenthood affiliates | U.S. communities |
| Teece (1980) | M-Form administrative structure | Industrial firms |
| Pitcher et al. (1978) | Collective violence | Countries |
| Oster (1982) | Basic oxygen furnace | Steel manufacturers |

distinct academic disciplines, including geography, sociology, economics, and education. Table 1.1 illustrates some of the diverse innovations the diffusion patterns of which have been systematically investigated in the past decade. The diffusion patterns of several other innovations are examined in detail in later sections.

**The S-Shaped Curve**

Although a wide variety of innovations and diffusion processes have been investigated, one research finding keeps recurring: If the cumulative adoption time path or temporal pattern of a diffusion process is plotted, the resulting distribution can generally be described as taking the form of an S-shaped (sigmoid) curve. Such a curve is depicted in Figure 1.1. The observed regularity in the diffusion process results from the fact that initially only a few members of the social system adopt the innovation in each time period. In subsequent time periods, however, an increasing number of adoptions per time period occur as the diffusion process begins to unfold more fully. Finally, the trajectory of the diffusion curve slows and begins to level off, ultimately reaching an upper asymptote. At this point diffusion is complete.

Although the diffusion pattern of most innovations can be described in terms of a general S-shaped curve, the exact form of each curve, including the slope and the asymptote, may differ. For example, the slope may be very steep initially, indicating rapid diffusion, or it may be gradual, indicating relatively slow diffusion.

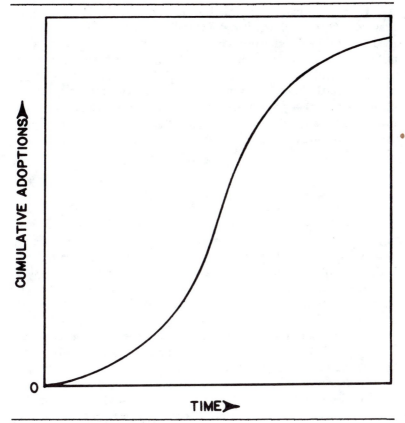

Figure 1.1    S-Shaped Diffusion Curve

Numerous hypotheses and interpretations have been set forth to explain the S-shaped nature of the diffusion curve. Mansfield (1961) hypothesized that the rate of diffusion is a function of the extent of economic advantage of the innovation, the amount of investment required to adopt the innovation and the degree of uncertainty associated with the innovation. Similarly, Griliches (1957), Robinson and Lakhani (1975), and Brown (1981) proposed a supply and demand rationale as a diffusion explanation. In contrast, Casetti and Semple (1969) and Sahal (1981) employed a learning perspective when explaining diffusion patterns; Hagerstrand (1967) and Bernhardt and MacKenzie (1972) offered an information transfer explanation.

An alternative explanation has been proposed by researchers such as Blackman (1974) and Sharif and Kabir (1976). These individuals have used a technological substitution frame of reference when interpreting diffusion processes. In particular, they hypothesized that because an innovation typically replaces an existing product, service, or technology (e.g., the substitution of synthetic fibers for natural fibers), the dynamics of this replacement process account for both the rate of the diffusion process and the shape of the diffusion curve. Finally, Rogers (1983) has offered a communications-based theory for interpreting the diffusion of diverse phenomena.

## Diffusion Models

Much of the early research on diffusion processes focused on describing observed diffusion patterns in terms of prespecified trend or distribution functions. For example, cumulative normal, Gompertz, and logistic distribution functions have all been used to model diffusion processes because each gives rise to an S-shaped curve.[1] However, because *any* unimodal distribution function will generate an S-shaped curve, it is often not possible to empirically determine which of several competing trend or distribution functions best describes a given diffusion curve. Therefore, attempts have been made to develop theory-based "diffusion models" for analyzing and modeling the spread of an innovation over time.

In particular, diffusion models have been developed to represent the level or spread of an innovation among a given set of prospective adopters in a social system in terms of a simple mathematical function of the time that has elapsed from the introduction of the innovation. The purpose of a diffusion model is to depict the successive increase in the number of adopters or adopting units over time. By doing so, a diffusion model permits prediction of the continued development of the diffusion process over time as well as facilitates a theoretical explanation of the dynamics of the diffusion process in terms of certain general characteristics. Interestingly enough, most diffusion models have their roots and analogues in models used to study epidemics in biology or life-death processes (e.g., Bailey, 1957; Pielou, 1969).

## A Need for Integration

Despite the wide usage and application of such models in a variety of diffusion and innovation settings, there is a paucity of information regarding their commonalities and distinguishing features. Moreover, there has been neither systematic discussion of their respective advantages nor guidelines provided to suggest their appropriate application when investigating the diffusion of an innovation. Consequently, existing diffusion models are often applied in an ad hoc, atheoretic manner, without regard to any conceptual framework.

Two decades ago, Katz et al. (1963: 240) remarked that "diffusion researchers in the several traditions which we have examined scarcely know of each other's existence." More recently, Kelly and Kranzberg (1978: 173) noted that:

> The perspectives and emphasis of the general diffusion research traditions are substantially different, but they are by and large not incompatible or in conflict. They are, in fact, implicitly—though rarely explicitly—complementary. The unexplained residue of one is often a major preoccupation of another.

Unfortunately, this state of affairs still exists. Despite an extensive diffusion literature, there still appears to be a "lack of diffusion" of research findings. Thus, although researchers in economics have a good understanding of what other researchers in their discipline are doing, they do not appear to be aware of analogous or relevant research being conducted in industrial engineering, sociology, or marketing, and vice versa. In brief, relatively few researchers have built upon prior research and information from disciplines other than their own when investigating the diffusion of an innovation.

By setting forth a number of widely used diffusion models, demonstrating their commonalities, and suggesting appropriate applications, this monograph will expose readers to a powerful set of techniques for investigating the temporal diffusion process of any innovation. A major goal is to stimulate readers to apply these diffusion models rather than "reinvent" techniques or use inappropriate techniques on an ad hoc basis. Hopefully, the discussion to follow will be beneficial to all researchers interested in the diffusion of innovations, regardless of their specific discipline or the particular innovation. Given the expository nature of this monograph, the discussion is limited to deterministic diffusion models.

**Structure of Presentation**

In the next chapter a "fundamental" deterministic diffusion model for analyzing the spread of an innovation over time is presented. The model is a "generalized" one in that it has been derived without reference to a specific technical, organizational, or social context. After a brief discussion of model formulation and concepts, several widely cited diffusion models are reviewed. In addition, the relationship between the fundamental model and distribution functions commonly used to model a diffusion process, such as the decaying exponential, logistic, and Gompertz, is discussed. Particular emphasis is placed upon interpreting the parameters of the fundamental diffusion model. Finally, both implicit and explicit assumptions underlying employment of the fundamental model are considered.

Chapter 3 consists of a discussion of "flexible" diffusion models. Analogous to Chapter 2, it begins with a description of selected underlying model concepts followed by various formulations and illustrations of flexible models. These models are pattern sensitive and consequently can accommodate a variety of diffusion patterns.

The fourth chapter describes certain advanced diffusion models and extensions to the fundamental model. Included in the section are discussions of dynamic diffusion models, multi-innovation diffusion models, space and time diffusion models, multistage diffusion models, multi-adoption diffusion models that directly incorporate influencing or change agents. Collectively, Chapters 3 and 4 depict state-of-the-art diffusion models. The fifth chapter contains illustrative applications of diffusion models in a variety of contexts. Its purpose is to convey both the generality and the power of the diffusion models presented. The final chapter briefly summarizes the material presented and provides conceptual insights as well as technical suggestions for the use of diffusion models.

The monograph also includes one appendix, which contains a brief derivation of a generalized, flexible diffusion model.

## 2. THE FUNDAMENTAL DIFFUSION MODEL

To apply and interpret the results of any diffusion model, one must first understand its conceptual as well as mathematical foundation. This, in turn, requires knowledge of the implicit as well as explicit assumptions underlying model formulation. Such knowledge can be obtained by first establishing the basic or fundamental diffusion model and then examining its major components and underpinnings.

The fundamental diffusion model can be expressed as the differential equation

$$\frac{d\,N(t)}{dt} = g(t)\,[\overline{N} - N(t)]$$ [1]

with the boundary condition

$$N(t = t_0) = N_0$$

where

N(t) = cumulative number of adopters at time t

$$(N(t) = \int_{t_0}^{t} n(t)dt, n(t)$$

being the noncumulative number of adopters at time t),

$\overline{N}$ = total number of potential adopters in the social system at time t,[2]

$\dfrac{d\,N(t)}{dt}$ = rate of diffusion at time t,

g(t) = coefficient of diffusion,

and

$N_0$ = cumulative number of adopters at time $t_0$.[3]

The diffusion model presented in equation 1 is a deterministic rate equation. It posits that the rate of diffusion of an innovation at any time t is a function of (that is, is directly proportional to) the gap or difference between the total number of possible adopters existing at that time and the number of previous adopters at that time $[\overline{N} - N(t)]$. A consequence of this model formulation is that as the cumulative number of prior adopters, N(t), approaches the total number of possible adopters in the social system, $\overline{N}$, the rate of diffusion decreases.

The form or nature of the relationship between the rate of diffusion and the number of potential adopters existing at t, $[\overline{N} - N(t)]$, is represented or controlled by g(t), the coefficient of diffusion. The specific value of g(t) depends on such characteristics of the diffusion process as the nature of the innovation, communication channels employed, and social system attributes.[4] In addition, g(t) can be interpreted as the probability of an adoption at time t. If this interpretation is used, then $g(t) \cdot [\bar{N} - N(t)]$ represents the expected number of adopters at time t, n(t). Furthermore, if n(t) is viewed as the number of social system members transferred from potential adopter status to adopter status at time t, then g(t) can also be considered a transfer mechanism, a conductivity coefficient or a coefficient of conversion.

Two distinct approaches have been used to represent g(t). One has been to represent g(t) as a function of time; the other has been to represent g(t) as a function of the number of previous adopters. Because the latter approach is by far the more common, it is the one employed here. Specifically, g(t) can be expressed as a function of N(t) such that

$$g(t) = a + b\ N(t) + c\ N(t)^2 + \ldots$$

However, for reasons such as convenience, a desire to retain analytical parsimony, and facilitation of interpretation and parameter estimation, g(t) has been typically formulated as either

$g(t) = a,$
$g(t) = b\ N(t),$ or
$g(t) = (a + b\ N(t)),$

where a and b are treated as model coefficients or parameters.

If g(t) = a, the fundamental diffusion model can be expressed as

$$\frac{d\ N(t)}{dt} = a\ [\bar{N} - N(t)] \qquad [2]$$

For pedagogical purposes, this version will be referred to as the *external-influence* diffusion model.

If g(t) = b N(t), the fundamental diffusion model can be expressed as

$$\frac{d\ N(t)}{dt} = b\ N(t)\ [\bar{N} - N(t)] \qquad [3]$$

This version will be referred to as the *internal-influence* diffusion model.

Finally, if g(t) = (a + b N(t)), the fundamental diffusion model can be expressed as

$$\frac{d\,N(t)}{dt} = (a + b\,N(t))\,[\bar{N} - N(t)] \tag{4}$$

In this version, the model will be referred to as the *mixed-influence* diffusion model because it simultaneously subsumes equations 2 and 3.

Each of these versions results in a diffusion curve the parameters of which possess both theoretical and practical interpretations and implications. For this reason, each of the three versions of the fundamental diffusion model is respectively examined below.[5]

## External-Influence Model

As noted above, in the external-influence diffusion model,

$$\frac{d\,N(t)}{dt} = a\,[\bar{N} - N(t)],$$

the constant term a is defined as an index or coefficient of *external* influence emanating from outside of the social system.[6] In general, a represents the influence of a "change agent(s)" on the diffusion process—any influence other than a prior adoption. Frequently a is interpreted as representing the effect of mass media communications on the diffusion process, although it has been used to represent the influence of government agencies, salespeople, and the like. Conceptually, a can be considered as representing the effect of a vertical channel(s) of communication, a centralized channel(s) of communication, a structured channel(s) of communication, or a formal channel(s) of communication.

Through elementary integration of equation 2 it is possible to derive the cumulative adopter distribution. Thus,

$$N(t) = \bar{N}\,[1 - \exp(-at)] \quad \text{or} \quad \ln\left[\frac{1}{\left(1 - \dfrac{N(t)}{\bar{N}}\right)}\right] = at$$

if $N(t = t_o = 0) = 0$.

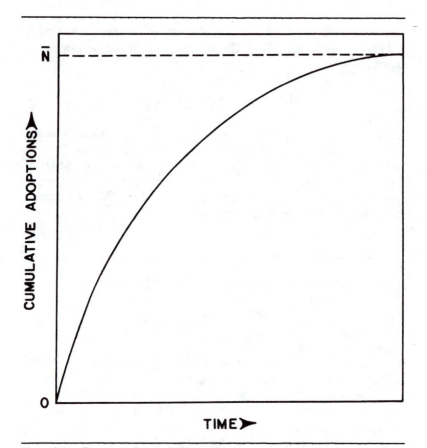

Figure 2.1    External-Influence Diffusion Curve

Much of the popularity of the external-influence model is due to the work of Coleman et al. (1966), who used it to investigate the diffusion of a new drug by physicians in four Midwestern communities. The model results in a decaying or modified exponential diffusion curve (i.e., the exponent is negative). The general shape of this curve is illustrated in Figure 2.1; over time the cumulative number of adopters increases, but at a (constant) decreasing rate. Diffusion processes with such a functional form are hypothesized as only being "driven" by information from a communication source external to the social system. Thus, applying this diffusion model requires the assumption that the rate of diffusion at time t is dependent only on the potential number of adopters present in the social system at time t. In other words, the model does not attribute any diffusion to interaction between prior adopters and potential adopters.

Application of the external-influence model has been illustrated by Hamblin et al. (1973). These researchers used the external-influence model to analyze "innovation" data representing, respectively, the number of labor strikes and political assassinations in 64 developing nations over a 20-year period. Because these nations were widely separated geographically, and the "innovations" were separated temporally, there was little evidence of communication or conspiracy among the strikers or assassins and, therefore, no interaction among social system members was assumed. Instead, it was hypothesized that the mass media—newspapers, radio, and magazines—were the only common channels of communication. In general, the external-influence model is appropriate when members of a social system are isolated (i.e., do not interact), as was true for certain physicians studied by Coleman et al. (1966), or for innovations that are not complex and/or subject to interpersonal communication (i.e., deviant behaviors or nonsocially conspicuous products), or when adequate information about the innovation is only available from a source(s) external to the social system.[7]

## Internal-Influence Model

Whereas the external-influence model is based on the assumption that there is no interpersonal communication among social system members, the internal-influence model

$$\frac{d\,N(t)}{dt} = b\,N(t)\,[\bar{N} - N(t)]$$

is based on a contagion paradigm such that diffusion occurs *only through* interpersonal contacts. In the internal-influence model, the rate of diffusion is treated solely as a function of interpersonal communication or social interaction between prior adopters and potential adopters in the social system. Interpersonal communication or social interaction is represented by $N(t) \cdot [\bar{N} - N(t)]$, (prior adopters) $\times$ (potential adopters). Hence, equation 3 can be considered as representing a *pure imitation* diffusion model.

The cumulative adopters distribution function of this model is derived as in the previous case by integration:

$$N(t) = \frac{\bar{N}}{1 + \dfrac{(\bar{N} - N_0)}{N_0} \exp\left[-b\,\bar{N}(t - t_0)\right]}$$

or

$$\ln\left[\frac{N(t)}{\bar{N} - N(t)}\right] = \ln\left[\frac{N_0}{(\bar{N} - N_0)}\right] + b\,\bar{N}(t - t_0)$$

where

$$N(t = t_0) = N_0.{}^{[8]}$$

This corresponds to a logistic diffusion curve such as that displayed in Figure 2.2.

The constant b is defined as an index of imitation or *internal* influence because it reflects the interaction of prior adopters $N(t)$ with potential adopters $(\bar{N} - N(t))$. Therefore, in contrast to a, b can be conceptualized as representing the effect of horizontal channels of communication, decentralized channels of communication, or unstructured, informal channels of communication.

Perhaps the most widely cited applications of the internal-influence model are those of Mansfield (e.g., 1961) and Griliches (e.g., 1957). Mansfield investigated the diffusion of several industrial innovations such as pallet loaders, diesel locomotives, and continuous mining machines among firms; Griliches studied the diffusion of hybrid seed corn in 31 states and 132 crop-reporting areas among farmers. Another frequently cited application of this model is Gray's (1973) investigation of the diffusion of 12 public policy innovations among the 48 contiguous United States.[9] The internal-influence model is most appropriate when an innovation is complex and socially visible, not adopting it places social system members at a "disadvantage" (e.g., a competitive disadvantage in business), the social system is relatively small and homo-

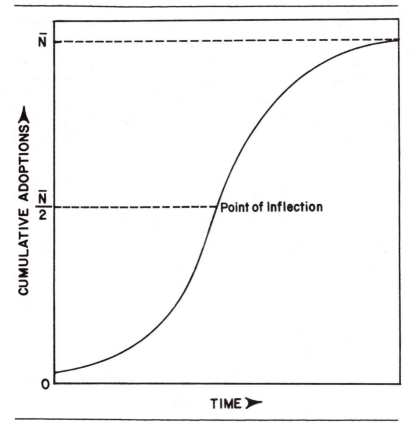

Figure 2.2    Internal-Influence Diffusion Curve

geneous, and there is a need for experiential or legitimizing information prior to adoption.

The internal-influence diffusion model is directly related to the well-known Gompertz function (see Figure 2.3), which is widely used in technological forecasting (e.g., Martino, 1983: chap. 4). Using the terminology of this section, the Gompertz function can be expressed as

$$\frac{d\,N(t)}{dt} = b\,N(t)\,[\ln \bar{N} - \ln N(t)]$$

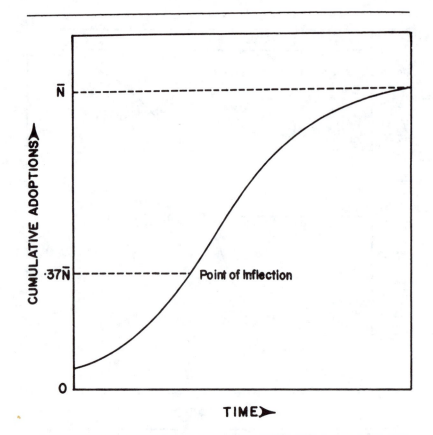

Figure 2.3    Gompertz Diffusion Curve

Assuming $N(t = t_0) = N_0$, the cumulative adopter distribution of the Gompertz function can be found through integration:

$$N(t) = \bar{N} \exp\left[-\left(\ln \frac{\bar{N}}{N_0}\right)\exp\left[-b\,(t-t_0)\right]\right]$$

or

$$\ln\left[\frac{\ln \bar{N} - \ln N(t)}{\ln \bar{N} - \ln N_0}\right] = -b\,(t-t_0)$$

Illustrative applications of the Gompertz function in a diffusion context include those of Hendry (1972), who modeled the sales growth of selected durable products in the United Kingdom, and Dixon (1980), who applied it to Griliches' hybrid seed corn data.[10]

## Mixed-Influence Model

The mixed-influence diffusion model,

$$\frac{d\,N(t)}{dt} = (a + b\,N(t))\,[\bar{N} - N(t)]$$

subsumes both of the previous models by incorporating parameters representing external as well as internal influences. As such, it is the most widely used and most general of the three fundamental diffusion model versions because it can accommodate the assumptions of the other two. (Seldom can the assumptions of either the external-influence or the internal-influence diffusion model alone be met unequivocally when investigating a diffusion process.) Integration of the mixed-influence model yields the following cumulative adopter distribution:

$$N(t) = \frac{\bar{N} - \dfrac{a(\bar{N} - N_0)}{(a + b\,N_0)}\ \exp\,[-(a + b\,\bar{N})\,(t - t_0)]}{1 + \dfrac{b(\bar{N} - N_0)}{(a + b\,N_0)}\ \exp\,[-(a + b\,\bar{N})\,(t - t_0)]}$$

where

$$N(t = t_0) = N_0.$$

Plotting the cumulative adopter distribution results in a generalized logistic curve, the shape of which is determined by both a and b. Most applications of the mixed-influence diffusion model have been concerned with forecasting the long-term sales of consumer durable products. The initial application of the mixed-influence diffusion model in this context was by Bass (1969), who used it to successfully forecast the sales of such products as television sets, dishwashers, and clothes dryers. Mahajan and Muller (1979) have provided a review and perspective of sales forecasting applications of the mixed-influence model.

The mixed-influence diffusion model has also been modified and used to investigate the impact of location (Webber, 1972: chap. 9), simulate the effect of certain internal and external influences on diffusion patterns (Lekvall and Wahlbin, 1973), forecast the market potential of a new solar technology (Warren, 1980), and study the diffusion of educational innovations (Lawton and Lawton, 1979). For example, when investigating the diffusion of six educational innovations, Lawton and Lawton (1979) set forth the following diffusion model:

$$\frac{d\,N(t)}{dt} = p^* \, \frac{N_0 + N(t)}{\bar{N} + N_0} \, [\bar{N} - N(t)]$$

where

$p^*$ = a diffusion rate parameter, and

$N_0$ = the "effective" number of initial adopters ($N_0$ is determined by solving the model as it takes the value of $N(t)$ at $t = 1$).

In this model, the coefficient of external influence, a, equals $p^* \, N_0/\bar{N} + N_0$ and the coefficient of internal influence, b, equals $p^*/\bar{N} + N_0$. Consequently, $a/b = N_0$ (a constant). Therefore, by specifying a relationship between the coefficients of external and internal influence, Lawton and Lawton (1979) were able to express differences in diffusion patterns in terms of a single rate parameter ($p^*$). In a subsequent paper Lawrence and Lawton (1981) have suggested that diffusion patterns can be generated a priori by setting $p^* = .66$ for industrial product innovations and $p^* = .50$ for consumer product innovations.

## Parameter Estimation Considerations

Application of any diffusion model involves estimating its parameters. In the absence of historical or time-series data, parameters can be estimated by means of certain innovation-specific analogues (Lawrence and Lawton, 1981) or expert judgments (Souder and Quaddus, 1982). If historical or time-series data are available, parameters can be estimated by means of standard but often nonlinear estimation procedures found in such sources as Draper and Smith (1981: chap. 10) or Oliver (1964; see also Srinivasan and Mason, 1984), or through maximum likelihood estimation procedures (e.g., Olson, 1982; Schmittlein and Mahajan, 1982). In ongoing diffusion processes in which relatively few data points are available, initial parameter values can be updated and revised as new data become available by using adaptive (Bretschneider and Mahajan, 1980) or Bayesian (Lilien et al., 1981) estimation procedures.

Although examples of some of these procedures are presented later, to complete this discussion of the fundamental diffusion model a simple procedure for obtaining model parameters suggested by Bass (1969) is briefly described below. For pedagogical ease, only the mixed-influence model is considered.

Because the mixed-influence model is essentially a 3-parameter model (a, b, and $\overline{N}$), parameter estimation requires time-series data on the number of adoptions in a minimum of three time periods.[11] Parameter estimation begins by rewriting the mixed-influence model

$$\frac{d\,N(t)}{dt} = (a + b\,N(t))\,[\overline{N} - N(t)]$$

in terms of its discrete analogue:

$$N(t + 1) - N(t) = a\,\overline{N} + (b\,\overline{N} - a)\,N(t) - b\,N^2(t)$$

$$= A_1 + A_2\,N(t) + A_3\,N^2(t) + e(t)$$

The A terms can then be evaluated numerically by means of ordinary least squares regression analysis and a, b, and $\overline{N}$ obtained as follows:

$$A_1 = a\,\overline{N} \ \text{ or } \ a = A_1/\overline{N}$$

$$A_3 = -b \ \text{ or } \ b = -A_3$$

and

$$\overline{N} = \frac{-A_2 \pm \sqrt{A_2^2 - 4\,A_1\,A_3}}{2A_3}$$

## Comment

Several assumptions that underlie the fundamental diffusion model must be recognized before it is applied or results are interpreted. For the most part, they are simplifying assumptions designed to facilitate analytical solutions to the model. One such assumption is that the diffusion process is *binary* (Sharif and Ramanathan, 1981). Members of a social system either adopt the innovation or they do not adopt it. Thus, adoption is treated as a discrete rather than continuous event. As a consequence of this assumption, the fundamental diffusion model does not take into account stages in the adoption process (e.g., awareness, knowledge, etc.).[12]

Second, the fundamental diffusion model is based on the assumption that there is a distinct and constant ceiling, $\overline{N}$, on the number of potential adopters in the social system and that this ceiling is either known or can be estimated. Simply stated, the size of the social system is deemed to be finite and fixed. Consequently, the fundamental diffusion model is *static*; the social system is not allowed to increase (grow) or decrease in size during the course of the diffusion process (Mahajan and Peterson, 1978; Sharif and Ramanathan, 1981).

Third, the fundamental diffusion model only permits one adoption by an adopting unit. Multiple adoptions by a single adopting unit (e.g., repeat purchasing of a product) are not permitted. A simultaneous assumption is that an adoption cannot be rescinded. There is no provision in the model for discontinuance of an innovation once it has been adopted.

Fourth, in the internal-influence and mixed-influence models, the term $N(t) [\overline{N} - N(t)]$ implies that there is complete mixing of social system members. In other words, it is assumed there is complete, pairwise interaction between prior adopters of an innovation and potential adopters. Furthermore, because

$$N(t) = \sum_{j=1}^{t} (N(j) - N(j-1)) = \sum_{j=1}^{t} n(j)$$

or

$$N(t) [\overline{N} - N(t)] = (n(1) + n(2) + \ldots + n(t)) [\overline{N} - N(t)]$$

it is implicitly assumed that the effect of interaction between prior and potential adopters (as reflected by the coefficient of internal influence, b) is identical, regardless of time of adoption and time of interaction. Hence, internal influence represented by $n(1)[\bar{N} - N(t)]$ is equivalent to that represented by $n(t)[\bar{N} - N(t)]$. Succinctly stated, the coefficient of internal influence is assumed to be temporally independent—fixed or constant over time. A related assumption is that the external-influence parameter a also does not change over the course of the diffusion process; it, too, is fixed or constant.

In addition, an implicit assumption is that the innovation itself does not change over the diffusion process. This means, for example, that in the case of a new technology, modifications would not take place during the diffusion process. Moreover, the innovation is assumed to be independent of other innovations. Thus, adoption of the innovation does not complement, substitute for, detract from, or enhance the adoption of any other innovation (and vice versa).

A sixth, implict assumption is that the geographical boundaries of the social system do not change over the diffusion process; the innovation is confined to one geographical area. In other words, the spatial diffusion of an innovation is not considered in the fundamental model.

Finally, when applying the fundamental diffusion model, a global assumption is that all relevant information about the diffusion process has been "captured" by the model. Thus, when forecasting the sales of a product, for example, it is assumed that all relevant information as to marketing strategies employed, activities of competitors, and the like is represented in the model, usually through the term $N(t)$. Generally speaking, application of the fundamental diffusion model requires the common forecasting assumption that the past can be used to predict the future.

## Example

Given these assumptions, there are relatively few "ideal" situations in which the fundamental diffusion model can be applied without caveats, restrictions, or extensions. Even so, in practice it frequently can be applied without deleterious consequences. One example is an analysis of the diffusion of public policy innovations among the continental United States by Mahajan et al. (1977). These researchers investigated the diffusion patterns (number and timing of adoptions) of several public policy innovations, three of which are illustrated here—accountant licensing, community affairs programs, and gasoline tax. In their application, the assumptions of a binary diffusion process, constant number of potential adopters (48), one adoption per unit (and no likely discontinuance),

**TABLE 2.1**
**Illustrative Results of Applying Mixed-Influence Diffusion Model**
**to Public Policy Adoptions by States**

| Public Policy | Time Span (Years) | Number of Adopters | Regression Constants | | | Diffusion Model Parameters | | |
|---|---|---|---|---|---|---|---|---|
| | | | $A_1$ | $A_2$ | $A_3$ | $a$ | $b$ | $\bar{N}$ |
| Accountant licensing | 1896-1951 | 48 | .1601 | 1.2678 | −.0058 | .0034 | .0058 | 48 |
| Community affairs programs | 1959-1970 | 36 | .0886 | 1.6065 | −.0147 | .0022 | .0147 | 41 |
| Gasoline tax | 1919-1929 | 48 | 3.4316 | 1.5757 | −.0141 | .0730 | .0141 | 48 |

SOURCE: Mahajan et al. (1977).

fixed geographical bounds, and complete mixing of social system members appeared reasonable. Table 2.1 contains selected results of their analysis based on a mixed-influence diffusion model incorporating both the a and b parameters. Interestingly enough, the model predicted there would be more adopters of community affairs programs than existed at the end of the data analysis period (1970). Details of the analysis are discussed in the original reference.

Because of the above assumptions and characteristics of the fundamental diffusion model, numerous refinements and extensions of it have been attempted. Several of the most useful are presented in the following chapters.

## 3. FLEXIBLE DIFFUSION MODELS

Although the fundamental diffusion model has been applied in a variety of contexts, its utility as a forecasting technique is increasingly being questioned. Bernhardt and Mackenzie (1972: 187), for example, have noted that in certain forecasting applications the fundamental diffusion model has functioned well although in other applications the results have been disappointing, suggesting that the success of many fundamental diffusion model applications has been due to "judicious choice of situation, population, innovation and time frame for evaluating the data." More recently, Heeler and Hustad (1980) reported examples of applications in which the mixed-influence diffusion model suggested by Bass (1969) did not perform well. Similar conclusions have been reached by Sharif and Islam (1980) and Schmittlein and Mahajan (1982).

This chapter reexamines the basic structure of the fundamental diffusion model in terms of two mathematical properties—point of inflection and symmetry. In practice as well as in theory, the maximum rate of diffusion of an innovation (the "point of inflection") should be able to occur at any time during the diffusion process. Additionally, diffusion patterns can be expected to be nonsymmetric as well as symmetric. However, both the internal-influence and the mixed-influence models at best offer only limited flexibility in terms of these two properties. (The external-influence model does not have a point of inflection.) Consequently, their ability to accommodate many diffusion patterns is restricted. This may partially explain why these models "work" in some applications but not in others. To overcome these deficiencies, several diffusion models are presented below that permit greater flexibility when modeling diffusion patterns.[13]

### Reexamination

The point of inflection on a diffusion curve occurs when the maximum rate of diffusion is reached. If the diffusion pattern after the point of inflection is the mirror image of the diffusion pattern before the point of inflection, the diffusion curve is characterized as being symmetric.

Consider the (logistic) internal-influence model, equation 3. If $F(t) = N(t)/\bar{N}$, the fraction of potential adopters that has adopted the innovation by time t, equation 3 can now be restated as (ignoring the subscript t for convenience):

$$\frac{dF}{dt} = bF(1-F) \qquad [5]$$

Integration of equation 5 yields

$$\ln \frac{F}{1-F} = c + bt$$

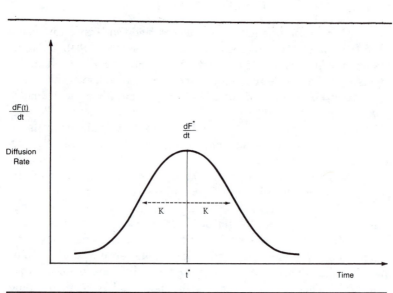

**Figure 3.1** Point of Inflection and Symmetry

where c is a constant equal to

$$\ln \frac{F_0}{1 - F_0} - bt_0 \text{ at } F(t = t_0) = F_0$$

The point of inflection for the internal-influence model can be obtained by differentiating equation 5 with respect to F, equating it to zero and solving for $F^*$. Doing so yields

$$\frac{d}{dF} [(bF(1 - F)] = 0 \text{ or } b(1 - 2F) = 0 \text{ or } F^* = 0.5$$

Hence, for the (logistic) internal-influence model, the maximum rate of diffusion is a constant that occurs when precisely 50% of the potential adopters have adopted the product.

In addition to possessing a fixed point of inflection, the logistic internal-influence diffusion curve is also symmetric because $dF/dt = b(1/4 - K^2)$ for $F = F^* + K$ as well as for $F = F^* - K$, where K is a constant fraction. This is illustrated graphically in Figure 3.1.

Similarly, the Gompertz formulation of the internal-influence diffusion model also possesses a fixed point of inflection (i.e., $F^* = 0.37$). Unlike the logistic internal-influence model, however, its diffusion curve is nonsymmetric. The mixed-influence diffusion model, on the other hand, generates a symmetric diffusion curve with a point of inflection that must occur when 50% or fewer of the potential adopters have adopted the innovation.

## Flexible Models

Because of the lack of flexibility of the fundamental diffusion model, several attempts have been made to develop more flexible diffusion models. Six of these models, for pedagogical purposes termed the Floyd model, the Sharif-Kabir model, the Jeuland model, the NSRL model, the NUI model, and the Von Bertalanffy model, are briefly described below. Each of these models is summarized in Table 3.1 with respect to the mathematical properties of inflection point and symmetry. For comparison purposes, the three versions of the fundamental diffusion model are also included in the table.[14]

### THE FLOYD MODEL

Floyd (1968) suggested the following flexible diffusion model in an attempt to empirically "fit" certain observed diffusion patterns:

$$\ln \frac{F}{1-F} + \frac{1}{1-F} = c + bt \qquad [6]$$

where c is a constant. If

$$F = F_0 \text{ at } t = t_0, \text{ then } c = \ln \frac{F_0}{1-F_0} + \frac{1}{1-F_0} - bt_0$$

Differentiation of equation 6 reveals that the Floyd model posits the rate equation

$$\frac{dF}{dt} = bF(1-F)^2$$

**TABLE 3.1**
**Selected Diffusion Model Characteristics**

| Model | Model Equation (dF/dt =) | Location of Point of Inflection (F*) | Symmetry |
|---|---|---|---|
| 1. Logistic Internal-Influence | $bF(1 - F)$ | 0.5 | S |
| 2. Gompertz Internal-Influence (e.g., Dixon, 1980) | $bF \ln \left( \dfrac{1}{F} \right)$ | 0.37 | NS |
| 3. Mixed-Influence (e.g., Bass, 1969) | $(a + bF)(1 - F)$ | 0.0-0.5 | S |
| 4. Floyd (1962) | $bF(1 - F)^2$ | 0.33 | NS |
| 5. Sharif-Kabir[1] (1976) | $\dfrac{bF(1 - F)^2}{1 - F(1 - \sigma)}$ | 0.33-0.5 | S or NS |
| 6. Jeuland[2] (1980) | $(a + bF)(1 - F)^{(1+\gamma)}$ | 0.0-0.5 | S or NS |
| 7. Non-Uniform Influence (NUI) (Easingwood et al., 1983) | $(a + bF^\delta)(1 - F)$ | 0.0-1.0 | S or NS |
| 8. Nonsymmetric Responding Logistic (NSRL) (Eastingwood et al., 1981) | $bF^\delta(1 - F)$ | 0.0-1.0 | S or NS |
| 9. Von Bertalanffy[3] (1957) | $\dfrac{b}{1 - \theta} F^\theta (1 - F^{(1-\theta)})$ | 0.0-1.0 | S or NS |

SOURCE: Adapted from Easingwood et al. (1983).
NOTE: S = symmetrical; NS = nonsymmetrical.
(1) $0 \leqslant \sigma \leqslant 1$; (2) $0 \leqslant \gamma$; (3) $0 \leqslant \theta$.

As summarized in Table 3.1 the Floyd model is nonsymmetric and possesses a fixed point of inflection at F* = 0.33. Hence, in these regards the Floyd model is similar to the Gompertz formulation of the internal-influence diffusion model.

**THE SHARIF-KABIR MODEL**

Sharif and Kabir (1976) have argued that by combining the internal-influence logistic model and the Floyd model, a smooth S-shaped curve within the region bounded by the two models can be obtained. Specifically, they proposed the model

$$(1 - \sigma) \left( \ln \frac{F}{1 - F} \right) + \sigma \left( \ln \frac{F}{1 - F} + \frac{1}{1 - F} \right) = c + bt \qquad [7]$$

or

$$\ln \frac{F}{1 - F} + \sigma \frac{1}{1 - F} = c + bt$$

where $\sigma$ is a constant and $0 \leq \sigma \leq 1$. If $\sigma = 0$, equation 7 reduces to the logistic internal-influence model; at $\sigma = 1$ it becomes the Floyd Model. Differentiation of equation 7 reveals that the Sharif-Kabir model implies the following rate equation:

$$\frac{dF}{dt} = \frac{bF(1 - F)^2}{1 - F(1 - \sigma)} \qquad [8]$$

Although the Sharif-Kabir model can accommodate symmetric as well as nonsymmetric diffusion patterns, it produces a point of inflection that must be in the range $0.33 \leq F \leq 0.5$.

### THE JEULAND MODEL

After analyzing the Bass (1969) mixed-influence diffusion model, Jeuland (1981) found that it implicitly assumed potential adopters were homogeneous with respect to their propensity to adopt.[15] Subsequently, he proposed a generalization of the Bass model based upon the following assumptions:

(1) external influence in the diffusion process relates to the potential adopter's propensity to adopt the innovation;
(2) the population of potential adopters is heterogeneous with respect to the propensity to adopt; and
(3) propensity to adopt varies according to a gamma distribution.

These assumptions led to the diffusion model

$$\frac{dF}{dt} = (a + bF)(1 - F)^{(1+\gamma)} \qquad [9]$$

When $\gamma = 0$, the Jeuland model reduces to the Bass mixed-influence model. When $a = 0$ and $\gamma = 1$, it reduces to the Floyd model. As can be seen in Table 3.1, although the Jeuland model can accommodate symmetric as well as nonsymmetric diffusion patterns, it cannot yield a point of inflection beyond a 50% adoption level.

**THE NSRL AND NUI MODELS**

Easingwood et al. (1981, 1983) proposed two flexible versions of the fundamental diffusion model. These are respectively termed the Nonsymmetric Responding Logistic (NSRL) model—a flexible internal-influence model—and the Non-Uniform Influence (NUI) model, a flexible mixed-influence model. The purpose of these models was to overcome an inherent limitation of the fundamental diffusion model—the assumption that the impact of internal influence between adopters and potential adopters remains constant over the entire diffusion process (i.e., the coefficient of internal-influence, $b$, is a time-invariant constant). For most innovations, this assumption is questionable because the impact of internal influence is likely to change, either increasing or decreasing, as the diffusion process unfolds. Easingwood et al. represented the impact of internal influence as a function of adoption level through the relationship

$$w(t) = bF^{\alpha}$$

where $\alpha$ is a constant and $w(t)$ represents the time-varying effect of internal influence. Hence, the flexible mixed-influence model (NUI) is:

$$\frac{dF}{dt} = (a + bF^{\delta})(1 - F) \qquad [10]$$

where $\delta = (1 + \alpha)$ and is referred to as the nonuniform influence factor. When $\delta = 1$ ( or $\alpha = 0$), the model assumes a constant or uniform internal influence. The presence of a nonuniform influence effect in the diffusion process is indicated by $\delta \neq 1$. When $a = 0$, the NUI model reduces to the flexible internal-influence diffusion model, the NSRL.

As shown in Table 3.1, the NUI and the NSRL models can both accommodate symmetric as well as nonsymmetric diffusion patterns. In addition, the point of inflection can occur at any time during the diffusion process.

It should be noted in passing that the other flexible diffusion models discussed so far implicitly assume the following representations for the effect of internal influence:

Floyd: $\quad w(t) = b(1 - F)$

Sharif-Kabir: $\quad w(t) = \dfrac{b(1 - F)}{(1 - F(1 - \sigma))}$

Jeuland: $\quad w(t) = b(1 - F)^{\gamma}$

However, in all of these models the effect of internal influence can only decrease with time. For the Sharif-Kabir model, differentiation of $w(t)$ with respect to F gives:

$$\frac{dw(t)}{dF} = \frac{-b\sigma}{(1 - F(1 - \sigma))^2}$$

Because b is positive and $0 \leqslant \sigma \leqslant 1$, $dw(t)/dF$ is negative and hence $w(t)$ must decrease with time. The same is true for the Jeuland model. Because

$$\frac{dw(t)}{dF} = -b\gamma(1 - F)^{\gamma - 1}$$

the effect of internal influence must decrease with time. Moreover, for all three models the internal influence effect becomes zero when F reaches unity. For the NUI or NSRL model, though,

$$\frac{dw(t)}{dF} = b(\delta - 1) F(t)^{\delta - 2}$$

is less than zero for $0 \leq \delta \leq 1$, equal to zero for $\delta = 1$, and greater than zero for $\delta > 1$. Because $dF/dt \geq 0$, the effect of internal influence can increase over time (when $\delta > 1$), remain constant ($\delta = 1$), or decrease ($0 < \delta < 1$); its value at complete adoption saturation is b. Hence, the time-varying nature of the effect of internal influence is described by a family of curves given by $bF^{\delta-1}$. In addition, values of $\delta$ between zero and one cause an acceleration of influence leading to an earlier and higher peak (i.e., $dF^*/dt$) in the level of adoptions. Values of $\delta$ greater than one reflect less internal influence and result in a later and lower peak. Unfortunately, despite their advantages, the NUI and NSRL models are not amenable to simple explicit solutions for F.

### THE VON BERTALANFFY MODEL

A relatively little-known diffusion model is the flexible model proposed by Von Bertalanffy (1957) and further articulated by Richards (1959). Because of its potential usefulness and a lack of familiarity with it in the innovation diffusion literature, mathematical details of this model are given in the Appendix. In essence, the model hypothesizes that

$$\frac{dF}{dt} = \frac{b}{1-\theta} F^{\theta}(1 - F^{(1-\theta)}) \qquad [11]$$

The fact that the Von Bertalanffy model is a flexible model can be demonstrated by examining its forms for various values of $\theta$. As shown in the Appendix, when $\theta = 0$, the model reduces to the external-influence model presented in Chapter 2. When $\theta = 2$, it is the traditional internal-influence model. Although the model breaks down at $\theta = 1$, it yields the Gompertz formulation of the internal-influence model as $\theta$ approaches one. Furthermore, as shown in Table 3.1, the Von Bertalanffy model accommodates both symmetric and nonsymmetric diffusion patterns with a point of inflection that can occur at any time during the diffusion process. Finally, the model can easily be extended to a mixed-influence diffusion model.

### Comment

Flexible diffusion models allow the generalized S-shaped diffusion curve to be symmetrical as well as nonsymmetrical, with the point of inflection responding to the diffusion pattern instead of being determined a priori. Although these models can be calibrated by means of the nonlinear or maximum likelihood procedures discussed in Chapter 2, they require estimation of an additional parameter. For example, in addition to a, b, and $\overline{N}$, the NUI model requires estimating $\delta$ and the Jeuland model requires estimating $\gamma$. Similarly, in addition to b and $\overline{N}$, the Sharif-Kabir, NSRL, and the Von Bertalanffy models require estimating $\sigma$, $\delta$, or $\theta$, respectively. Hence, all flexible diffusion models achieve their flexibility by requiring estimation of an additional parameter. As a consequence of their flexible nature, though, it is possible to develop a taxonomy of diffusion patterns because the models produce diffusion curves that mirror, rather than "force" the shape of the underlying diffusion data.

Despite the increased flexibility for capturing diffusion patterns, flexible models are also characterized by the same seven assumptions underlying the fundamental diffusion models. The next chapter presents diffusion models that address some of these assumptions.

## 4. EXTENSIONS AND REFINEMENTS

In Chapter 2 several assumptions underlying the fundamental diffusion model were set forth. Although these assumptions are necessary to derive analytical solutions to the model, they restrict its theoretical as well as practical application. To recapitulate, the assumptions are that (1) the diffusion process is binary, (2) there is a fixed ceiling on the number of potential adopters, (3) there is only one adoption by an adopting unit, (4) there is a complete mixing of prior and potential adopters with model parameters constant over the diffusion process, (5) the innovation is independent of all other innovations, (6) the geographical boundaries of the social system do not change over the diffusion process, and (7) all relevant information about the diffusion process has been "captured" by the model.

This section reviews extensions and refinements of the fundamental diffusion model. The review is not comprehensive, but rather highlights efforts that have been made to overcome some of the inherent limitations of the fundamental model by "relaxing" certain model assumptions. Included in this section are discussions of dynamic diffusion models, multi-innovation diffusion models, space and time diffusion models, multistage diffusion models, multiadoption diffusion models, and diffusion models that incorporate influencing or change agents. As such, the models presented in this chapter complement those in Chapter 3.

## Dynamic Diffusion Models

Succinctly stated, the fundamental diffusion model assumes that the ceiling on the number of potential adopters in a social system, $\overline{N}$, is static or fixed at the time an innovation is introduced and remains constant over the diffusion process. Thus, if the innovation is a product, for example, this implies that the market potential of the product is determined at the time of introduction ($t_0$) and remains unchanged over its entire life. Obviously such an assumption is not tenable with regard to either theory or practice. From a theoretical perspective, there is no rationale for a static potential adopter population. Instead, a potential adopter population continuously in flux is to be expected. Likewise, in practice a common objective is to continuously increase the "pool" of potential adopters of an innovation.

If the fundamental diffusion model were applied to a diffusion process that is *dynamic*, incorrect parameter estimates and/or incorrect forecasts may result to the extent that $\overline{N}$ fluctuates. In response to this shortcoming Mahajan and Peterson (1978) proposed a dynamic diffusion model wherein $\overline{N}$ is permitted to vary over time. In particular, they specified

$$\overline{N}(t) = f(\underline{S}(t))$$

where $\underline{S}(t)$ is a vector of (potentially) relevant exogenous and endogenous variables—controllable as well as uncontrollable—affecting $\overline{N}(t)$. Thus, if $f(\underline{S}(t))$ is substituted for $\overline{N}$ in equation 4, a dynamic mixed-influence model results:

$$\frac{dN(t)}{dt} = (a + b\,N(t))\,[f(\underline{S}(t)) - N(t)] \qquad [12]$$

The solution to equation 12 is[16]

$$N(t) = -\frac{a}{b} + \frac{\exp\left\{a(t - t_0) + b\,\phi(t)\right\}}{\left(\dfrac{b}{a + bN_0}\right) + b \displaystyle\int_{t_0}^{t} \exp\left\{a(x - t_0) + b\phi(x)\right\} dx}$$

where

$$N(t = t_0) = N_0 \text{ and } \phi(t) = \int_{t_0}^{t} f(\underline{S}(x))dx \qquad [13]$$

It should be reiterated that equation 12 reduces to equation 4 when $\overline{N}(t) = f(\underline{S}(t)) = \overline{N}$. Examples of relevant variables include socioeconomic conditions in the social system, increases or decreases in the population of the social system, government actions, efforts to influence the diffusion process (e.g., advertising), and so forth.

Figure 4.1 depicts the diffusion curve of an innovation when $\overline{N}$ is increasing over time. The following features of the dynamic model are illustrated by the figure:

(1) The ceiling on the number of potential adopters $(\overline{N})$ is increasing over time, and its curve is distinctly different from the diffusion curve of the innovation $(N(t))$, especially during early stages of the diffusion process.

(2) The difference between the ceiling on the number of potential adopters and the actual cumulative number of adopters decreases with time and, ultimately, the two curves coincide.[17]

Which or how many variables to incorporate into $\underline{S}(t)$ is a function of several factors, both conceptual and pragmatic. The nature of the innovation being investigated is a limiting factor, as is the availability of relevant data. Needless to say, the accuracy of the dynamic diffusion model in part depends upon identifying variables for $\underline{S}(t)$ that are closely related to or affect $\overline{N}(t)$. For example, if $\overline{N}(t)$ is expressed in terms of social system growth, the accuracy of the dynamic model is influenced by the accuracy of the growth forecasts. Similarly, the functional form of $f(\underline{S}(t))$ may vary across model applications.

Mahajan and Peterson (1978) applied their dynamic diffusion model to membership in the United Nations during the period 1945-1974. Because the number of countries in the world nearly doubled over this time period, the ceiling on the number of potentially joining countries (adopters) definitely was not static. Although a number of factors (e.g., geopolitical) could have affected adoption (joining), only the number of countries existing each year during the investigation period was used to define $\overline{N}$. In their application $\overline{N}(t)$ was first modeled using the fundamental diffusion model to estimate the cumulative number of countries

38

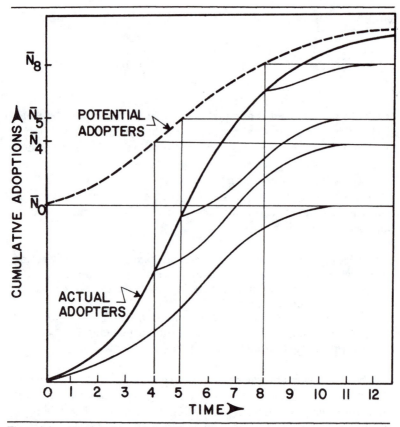

Figure 4.1    Dynamic Innovation Diffusion Pattern

$(P(t))$ in the world for the years 1945-1974. Then $\overline{N}(t)$ was related to $P(t)$ through the formulation:

$$\overline{N}(t) = f(P(t)) = K_1 + K_2\, P(t)$$

In general, the dynamic diffusion model performed quite well. Parameter values were theoretically correct as to their signs and magnitudes and the degree of model fit was satisfactory.[18]

Other dynamic diffusion models have been developed by Chow (1967), Lackman (1978), Dodson and Muller (1978) and Sharif and Ramanathan (1981).[19] Examining the natural growth of computers by means of a Gompertz internal-influence model, Chow argued that the number of computer adoptions was influenced by a "technological change-price reduction" effect. He implicitly assumed the following formulation to represent this effect:

$$\overline{N}(t) = B_0(P(t))^{-B_1}$$

where $B_0$ and $B_1$ are constants and $P(t)$ is computer price. Similarly, Lackman (1978) used a Gompertz-based dynamic model formulation when studying the growth of a new plastic product in the automotive industry:

$$\overline{N}(t) = \overline{N}\left(\frac{ZB(t)}{Sc(t)}\right)^K$$

where K is a constant, $ZB(t)$ represents corporate profits and $Sc(t)$ denotes corporate sales. The profit-sales variable was included to reflect the fact that users shift to new products quickly when profitability is high. The Dodson-Muller and Sharif-Ramanathan models are described later in more detail in a different context.

## Multi-Innovation Diffusion Models

Innovations are neither introduced into a vacuum nor do they exist in isolation. Other innovations exist in the social system and may have an influence—either positive or negative—on the diffusion of an innovation. In particular, Peterson and Mahajan (1978) have identified four categories of innovation interrelationships that can affect the adoption rate as well as the cumulative number of adoptions of an innovation. Innovations may be:

(1) Independent—innovations are independent of each other in a functional sense, but adoption of one may enhance adoption of others (e.g., modular housing units and electric trash compactors).
(2) Complementary—increased adoptions of one innovation result in increased adoptions of other innovations (e.g., washers and dryers).
(3) Contingent—adoption of one innovation (e.g., computer software) is conditional on (usually previous) adoption of other innovations (e.g., computer hardware).

(4) Substitutes—increased adoptions of one innovation result in decreased adoptions of other innovations (e.g., black and white versus color television sets).

They extended the fundamental mixed-influence diffusion model to represent all four categories of innovation interrelationships. For example, they expressed a *substitution* relationship between two innovations by the following rate equations:[20]

$$\frac{dN_1(t)}{dt} = (a_1 + b_1 N_1(t) - c_1 N_2(t)) [\bar{N}_1 - N_1(t)] \qquad [14]$$

and

$$\frac{dN_2(t)}{dt} = (a_2 + b_2 N_2(t) - c_2 N_1(t)) [\bar{N}_2 - N_2(t)] \qquad [15]$$

Equation 14 refers to one innovation, and equation 15 refers to the other. In these equations $c_1$ and $c_2$ represent the hypothesized substitution effect of the innovations on each other. Thus, equation 14 may be rewritten as

$$\frac{dN_1(t)}{dt} = a_1 [\bar{N} - N_1(t)] + b_1 N_1(t) [\bar{N}_1 - N_1(t)]$$

$$- c_1 N_2(t) [\bar{N}_1 - N_1(t)] \qquad [16]$$

The term in equation 16 that contains the constant $c_1$ represents an interaction between the adopters of innovation 2 and nonadopters of innovation 1; it results in a decrease in the rate of diffusion for innovation 1.

Multi-innovation diffusion models can easily be used to test hypothesized relationships between innovations. For example, when comparing the sales growth rates of color and black and white television sets from 1959 to 1973, Peterson and Mahajan (1978) found that although a substitution-model specification was not appropriate for color television sets, it improved model fit for black and white television sets significantly. In other words, substitution was unidirectional: The growth in sales of color television sets had a substitution effect on the sales growth of black and white television sets although the converse was not true. If anything, the sales growth of black and white television sets slightly *complemented* that of color sets.

Other researchers have addressed the nature of innovation interdependencies in the context of "competitive independence." This is the notion that an innovation is only offered by a single organization or, if more than one organization does offer it, the organizations' innovation offerings have no impact on each other. Examples of research refuting this notion, in the area of business, include the work of Eliashberg and Jeuland (1982), Rao and Bass (1984), Clarke and Dolan (1984), Mate (1982), Teng and Thompson (1983), and Fershtman et al. (1983). The major thrust of these cited works seems to be toward examination of pricing or advertising strategies of the competing firms and their impact on "market equilibrium."

## Space and Time Diffusion Models

In spite of the fact that the diffusion of any innovation occurs simultaneously in space and time, research on these two "dimensions" of diffusion has seldom been integrated. Although the time dimension has been investigated by researchers representing a wide variety of disciplines, spatal diffusion has, for the most part, only been investigated by geographers (Brown, 1981). Most geographical-based research on diffusion has been directed toward the development and refinement of Monte Carlo simulation models to implement the diffusion-process conceptualization initially proposed by Hagerstrand (1967). He viewed diffusion as the transformation of a population from one with a low proportion of adopters to one with a high proportion of adopters by means of information disseminated through mass media and interpersonal contact. In his investigations he identified three empirical regularities: An S-shaped curve, a hierarchical effect (diffusion is expected to proceed from larger to smaller centers), and a neighborhood effect (diffusion is expected to proceed in wavelike fashion outward from an urban center, first progressing to nearby rather than remote locations).

One attempt to address diffusion from a joint space and time perspective is that of Mahajan and Peterson (1979). They extended the fundamental mixed-influence diffusion model to integrate the space and time dimensions of the diffusion process. In so doing, they suggested that, in a forecast context, a diffusion agency may be interested not only in estimating "aggregate" adoptions of an innovation, but also in assessing how the innovation is diffusing in different geographical regions. This information would enable the agency to compare adoption rates and numbers of adoptions in different regions, as well as assess the feasibility of introducing the innovation in other regions and determine appropriate introduction strategies for doing so. Although a possible approach for estimating adoptions in multiple regions is to develop independent diffusion models for each one, such an aproach is inefficient. It requires development of numerous diffusion models and ignores the "richness" of regional interactions.

In their space and time extension, Mahajan and Peterson (1979) utilized two of the three empirical regularities identified in the spatial diffusion literature—the S-shaped curve and the neighborhood effect. They first assumed that growth in the number of adoptions in each region could be represented by a mixed-influence diffusion model with its unique a, b, and $\bar{N}$ parameters. Second, they assumed the relative number of adoptions would be greater in those regions closest to the region of innovation origination.[21]

Figure 4.2 illustrates the simultaneous diffusion of an innovation in space and time. In the figure, spatial diffusion has been oversimplified by reducing it to a single directional coordinate with the innovation being introduced into only one region.

Mahajan and Peterson made a similar simplification in that they assumed an innovation is first introduced into only one region, and the distance, x, between the innovative region and the remaining regions could be measured from the central distribution point of one region to another. This resulted in the following formulation of the space-time model:

$$N = f(x, t); \quad \frac{\partial N}{\partial y} = 0 \qquad [17]$$

or

$$\frac{\partial N(x, t)}{\partial t} = (a(x) + b(x) N(x, t)) \, [\bar{N}(x) - N(x, t)] \qquad [18]$$

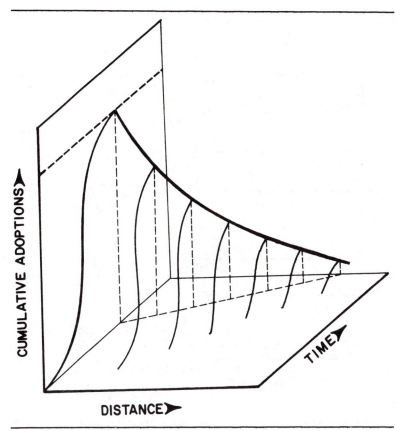

Figure 4.2    Space-Time Innovation Diffusion

and

$$N(x,t) = \frac{\bar{N}(x) - \dfrac{a(x)(\bar{N}(x) - N_0(x))}{a(x) + b(x)N_0(x)} \exp\left(-(a(x) + b(x)\bar{N}(x))(t - t_0)\right)}{1 + \dfrac{b(x)(\bar{N}(x) - N_0(x))}{a(x) + b(x)N_0(x)} \exp\left(-(a(x) + b(x)\bar{N}(x))(t - t_0)\right)} \quad [19]$$

To illustrate their model, Mahajan and Peterson reanalyzed data documenting the adoption of tractors in 25 states in the central agricultural production region of the United States for the period 1920-1964

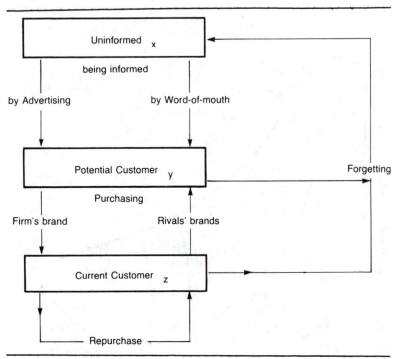

**Figure 4.3** Flow Diagram of Multistage Innovation Diffusion Process Model (Dodson and Muller, 1978)

(Casetti and Semple, 1969). In constructing their model they assumed $N(x) = (K_1 - K_2 X^2/2)$, where $K_1$ and $K_2$ are constants. The model fitted the data quite well; all parameter values were statistically significant.[22]

## Multistage Diffusion Models

The diffusion models presented in Chapters 2 and 3 are essentially two-stage or binary models. That is, they primarily consider the flow of social system members from potential adopters to current adopters. As articulated by Rogers (1983: 165), in practice, however, an adopting unit may pass through a series of stages in the innovation-decision process. Some of the attempts made to extend two-stage models to incorporate the multistage (or polynomial) nature of the diffusion process include models suggested by Midgley (1976), Dodson and Muller (1978), Sharif and Ramanathan (1982) and Mahajan, Muller, and Kerin (1984).

Figure 4.3, for example, presents the three-stage model proposed by Dodson and Muller (1978). The model hypothesizes that because of advertising and word-of-mouth influence, uninformed social system members first become potential adopters (customers) and then current adopters (customers). In the presence of competing innovations (e.g., brands), current adopters can either readopt (repurchase) the same innovation or by adopting competing innovations return to potential adopter status. Finally, because of forgetting, current adopters and potential adopters can become members of the uninformed group.

To motivate the discussion mathematically, consider Figure 4.3 without repurchase and forgetting (these features are treated later under the topic of multiadoption models). Let $x(t)$ = number of social system members who are unaware of the innovation at time t, $y(t)$ = number of social system members who are aware of the innovation at time t but still have not adopted it and, $z(t)$ = number of current adopters who have adopted the innovation. If it is assumed that the total population of the social system M remains constant over time, then at any time t

$$x(t) + y(t) + z(t) = M$$

or

$$\frac{dx(t)}{dt} + \frac{dy(t)}{dt} + \frac{dz(t)}{dt} = 0$$

or

$$\frac{dx(t)}{dt} = -\frac{dy(t)}{dt} - \frac{dz(t)}{dt} \qquad [20]$$

Thus, the Dodson-Muller model requires specification of only two rate equations to describe the flow of social system members in the diffusion process. More specifically, tracking the inflows and outflows across the three stages in Figure 4.3, the model can be written as (ignoring subscript t for convenience):

$$\frac{dy}{dt} = \beta x(y + z) + \mu x - \gamma y \qquad [21]$$

$$\frac{dz}{dt} = \gamma y \qquad [22]$$

The first term in equation 21 indicates the increase in the number of potential adopters due to the interaction between uninformed social system members and potential and current adopters; the second term, $\mu x$, represents the increase due to external influences (i.e., advertising). The third term, $\gamma y$, denotes the decrease in the number of potential adopters due to the transfer of potential adopters to current adopters. As indicated by equation 20, summation of equations 21 and 22 gives the decrease in the number of the uniformed social system members. Note that the Dodson-Muller model uses a mixed-influence approach to represent the flow of uninformed social system members to potential adopters and the external-influence model to represent the flow of potential adopters to current adopters. In order to show the linkage between the binary models presented in Chapters 2 and 3 and the multistage model proposed by Dodson and Muller, note that $x = M - \bar{N}(t)$, $y = \bar{N}(t) - N(t)$, and $z = N(t)$. Hence, equations 21 and 22 can be written as follows:

$$\frac{d}{dt}(\bar{N}(t) - N(t)) = \beta\bar{N}(t)(M - \bar{N}(t)) + \mu(M - \bar{N}(t))$$

$$-\gamma(\bar{N}(t) - N(t)) \qquad [21a]$$

$$\frac{dN(t)}{dt} = \gamma(\bar{N}(t) - N(t)) \qquad [22a]$$

or

$$\frac{d\bar{N}(t)}{dt} = \beta\bar{N}(t)(M - \bar{N}(t)) + \mu(M - \bar{N}(t)) \qquad [21b]$$

$$\frac{dN(t)}{dt} = \gamma(\bar{N}(t) - N(t)) \qquad [22b]$$

Thus, by assuming a three-stage process, the Dodson-Muller model specifies that the ceiling $\bar{N}$ in the external-influence diffusion model, equation 22b, varies with time according to the mixed-influence model, equation 21b.

The multistage diffusion model of Dodson and Muller, as well as the basic models presented in Chapters 2 and 3, implicitly assumes that an individual's experience with the innovation is communicated positively through word-of-mouth. This assumption is tenuous because communi-

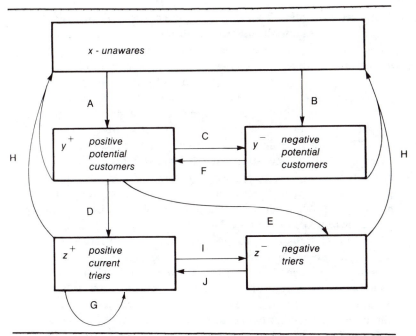

Figure 4.4    Customer Flow Diagram for Product Innovations in Which Both Positive and Negative Types of Information are Circulated (Mahajan et al., 1984)

cators of the innovation experience may transfer favorable, unfavorable, or indifferent messages to others. The multistage models proposed by Midgley (1976), Sharif and Ramanathan (1982) and Mahajan et al. (1984) attempt to relax this assumption in their formulations. Figure 4.4, for example presents the multistage model suggested by Mahajan et al. (1984). An extension of the Dodson-Muller model, this model divides the potential adopters (customers) and current adopters (triers) into two groups, each based on the positive or negative nature of communicated information.[23] Mahajan et al. have applied their model to forecast attendance for the movie "Gandhi" in the Dallas, Texas area.

## Multiadoption Diffusion Models

As defined in Chapter 1, the objective of a diffusion model is to represent the level or spread of an innovation among a given set of prospective adopters. That is, the purpose of the model is to depict the successive increase in the number of adopters. In a product-innovation context, however, the successive increase in the number of adopters may consist of first-time buyers as well as repeat buyers of an innovation. Because a great many product-innovations that are introduced into the marketplace are repurchasable, sellers of these innovations are interested in predicting the successive increase in number of adopters due to repeat buyers even more than the number of first-time buyers. It has been frequently determined that repeat buyers tend to become heavy users of a product-innovation given their satisfactory experience with it at the trial (initial adoption) stage. Therefore, it is the continued repurchase of the product that creates a successful innovation. In brief, for nonrepurchasable product-innovations (e.g., many consumer durables), the purpose of a diffusion model is to depict the first-purchase diffusion curve. For repurchasable products (e.g., packaged goods), however, the purpose is also to model the repeat purchase diffusion curve.

A number of repeat-purchase models have been developed to forecast sales for product-innovations (for a comprehensive review of these models, see Wind et al., 1981). Most of these models use consumer purchase and/or survey data collected at a pretest or test market stage to develop first-purchase and repeat-purchase sales forecasts. Furthermore, as indicated by Mahajan and Muller (1982) in their review of eleven such models, most of these models exclude the effect of word-of-mouth communication in their formulations.

Two diffusion models that use early diffusion data and explicitly consider word-of-mouth communication in their formulations to forecast repeat purchase, have been proposed, respectively, by Lilien et al. (1981) and Mahajan et al. (1983). In addition to these two models, for comparison purposes the repeat-purchase model suggested by Dodson and Muller (1978) is also discussed here (see Figure 4.3). Calibration of the latter model, however, requires purchase data from a consumer panel.

The models suggested by Lilien et al. (1981) and Mahajan et al. (1983) were developed to forecast the sales of ethical drugs. Using the notation of Chapters 2 and 3, in general, they can be summarized as follows (see the original references for details):

$$N(t + 1) = a(t)(\bar{N} - N(t)) + b(N(t) - N(t - 1))(\bar{N} - N(t))$$

$$+ c(t)N(t) \tag{23}$$

$$N(t + 1) = a(\bar{N} - N(t)) + b \left(\frac{N(t)}{\bar{N}}\right)^{\delta} (\bar{N} - N(t)) + cN(t) \qquad [24]$$

Equation 23 represents the repeat-purchase model of Lilien et al. (1981); equation 24 is the model proposed by Mahajan et al. (1983). Some comments about these two models are warranted.

(1) The model proposed by Mahajan et al. (1983) is a direct extension of the NUI model discussed in Chapter 3. Assuming a constant population of potential adopters, the first term in equation 24 represents the number of adopters at time $(t + 1)$ due to external influence, the second term denotes adopters due to word-of-mouth communication, and the third indicates the fraction of adopters in period t who continue to adopt in period $(t + 1)$. Hence, the constant c is an index or coefficient of retention.

(2) The model developed by Lilien et al. (1981) also contains three terms. However, in their application of the model to forecast the sales of ethical drugs, they represented the coefficient of external influence, a, as a function of a firm's promotional (e.g., detailing) efforts and the coefficient of retention, c, as a function of competitors' promotional (detailing) efforts. With regard to the interaction effect (the second term), because $N(t)$ can be greater than or less than $N(t-1)$, they assume that at any time t the number of potential adopters, $(\bar{N} - N(t))$, can be influenced only by the additional number of adopters who adopt between time t and $(t - 1)$—as compared to *all* of the adopters, $N(t)$, as assumed in equation 24—or those who *stop* repurchasing the product between time t and $(t - 1)$ as reflected by $(N(t) - N(t - 1))$.

The complete Dodson-Muller model, Figure 4.3, also includes repeat purchasing and forgetting. Because they assumed a constant population of the social system, as indicated earlier, their flow diagram can be represented by two rate equations. In fact, as derived by Mahajan et al. (1983), their repeat-purchase model can be written as follows:

$$N(t + 1) = \gamma(\bar{N}(t) - N(t)) + cN(t) \qquad [25]$$

$$\bar{N}(t) = \mu(M - \bar{N}(t - 1)) + \beta\bar{N}(t - 1)(M - \bar{N}(t - 1)) + K\bar{N}(t - 1) \qquad [26]$$

where $c = 1 - \phi - \theta$ and $K = 1 - \theta$. The parameter $\phi$ is a constant forgetting factor and $\theta$ is a constant switching factor reflecting adoption of a competitive product. This model is also a straightforward extension of their first-purchase model, equations 21 and 22.

The diffusion rate equation 25 contains two terms. The first reflects adopters due to external influence and the second reflects adopters at time t who continue to repurchase at time (t + 1). Because $cN(t) = N(t) - \phi N(t) - \theta N(t)$, the number of repurchasers at time (t + 1) is obtained by substracting the number of social system members who forget about the product, $\phi N(t)$, and the number who switch to a competitive product, $\theta N(t)$, from $N(t)$. The dynamic market potential, $\bar{N}(t)$, in equation 26 includes newly awares due to advertising (first term), newly awares due to word-of-mouth (second term) and potential adopters who do not switch over to a competitive product as reflected by $K = 1 - \theta$.

The three repeat-purchase diffusion models do not distinguish between repeat adopters in terms of the number of times they have repurchased the product. That is, the models ignore the "depth" of repeat buying; they do not distinguish between first repeaters, second repeaters, and so on.

## Diffusion Models with Influencing/Change Agents

The major criticism of the basic diffusion models presented in Chapters 2 and 3 is that they are of little use to agencies interested in diffusing an innovation because they consider diffusion as a function of time only. The strategies employed by an agency to diffuse an innovation are not explicitly included in the models, thus inhibiting evaluation of the effect of different strategies on innovation diffusion.

Because most diffusion models essentially contain three parameters (coefficients of external influence and internal influence, and the total number of potential adopters) diffusion strategies may be directly incorporated into these models by representing the parameters as functions of relevant variables, for example:

$$a(t) = A(\underline{S}(t))$$
$$b(t) = B(\underline{S}(t))$$
$$\bar{N}(t) = \bar{N}(\underline{S}(t))$$

Previously it was noted that some attempts have been made to represent the ceiling, $\bar{N}$, as a function of exogenous and endogenous variables.

To reiterate, Dodson and Muller (1978) represented N as a function of advertising. Mahajan and Peterson (1978) and Sharif and Ramanathan (1981) treated it as a function of social system population growth estimates. Chow (1967) evaluated $\overline{N}$ as a function of price, and Lackman (1978) investigated the growth of a new plastic in the automotive industry by representing $\overline{N}$ as a function of the ratio between corporate profits and corporate sales.

Other attempts to incorporate diffusion strategies, mainly by economists, technological forecasters, and marketing researchers, have been concerned with representing the coefficients of external influence and internal influence as functions of diffusion-influencing variables. Motivated by the work of Mansfield (1961), economists and technological forecasters have studied the diffusion (or substitution) of technological innovations by representing the coefficient of internal influence as a function of profitability and investment. That is,

$$b = z - b_1 \pi - b_2 I$$

where $z$ = a constant representative of a given industry, $\pi$ = a profitability index, and $I$ = an investment index. The general conclusion seems to be that the more profitable the innovation and the smaller the required investment, the greater the rate of diffusion. An illustrative application of this approach by Randles (1983) is discussed in Chapter 5.

Marketing researchers have concentrated on the roles of pricing, advertising, promotion, and technological change on the diffusion process. Robinson and Lakhani (1975), for example, noted that because a has been found to be very small for consumer durables, b should be developed as a function of marketing decision variables. They argued that innovators are a dominant factor in the marketplace only during the short period required to achieve initial market penetration. Therefore, if b is developed as a function of marketing decision variables such as advertising, promotion, and price, the basic diffusion models will enable management to evaluate their effect on the diffusion of a product-innovation.

Representing b as a function of price only, that is,

$$b = \overline{b} \exp(-ep)$$

where $\overline{b}$ and e are constants and p is unit price, Robinson and Lakhani (1975) used the Bass mixed-influence model to illustrate the effect of price on the profitability of a new product. Their work led Bass (1980),

Dolan and Jeuland (1981), Jorgenson (1983), and Kalish (1983) to further examine the relationship between pricing policies and diffusion rates.

The approach of Horsky and Simon (1983) differs from that of Robinson and Lakhani (1975). First, Horsky and Simon concluded that marketing activities such as price changes and product modifications are more likely to affect the eventual number of adopters, $\overline{N}$, than a or b. They hypothesized that due to increased competition and decreases in production costs as a result of learning, substantial price reductions can be expected in a new product during the early stage of its life cycle. These reductions will place the product within the reach of a great number of potential buyers, thus expanding the eventual number of adopters, $\overline{N}$. Regarding changes in the nature of the product, they believed that firms will tailor their products to different market segments as the interests of those segments become apparent. One consequence of this tailoring is to expand the eventual number of adopters, $\overline{N}$.

Second, to incorporate advertising into their diffusion model, Horsky and Simon (1983) suggested that to be correctly specified a diffusion model should include advertising as a source of information to innovators. In other words, a instead of b should be expressed as a function of advertising (expenditures). An increase in advertising in the initial period of diffusion will facilitate the overall diffusion process by informing possible innovators about the existence of the product and thereby turn them into word-of-mouth carriers. This in turn will cause the peak in sales to be higher and to occur earlier than if such advertising did not exist. Consequently, expressing b as a function of advertising will only result in a second-order effect.

Although Horsky and Simon (1983) appreciated the idea of a dynamic market potential, they assume constant values of $\overline{N}$ and b but assume that

$$a = \overline{a}_1 + \overline{a}_2 \ln A$$

where $\overline{a}_1$ and $\overline{a}_2$ are constants and A is the level of advertising expenditures at time t.

Horsky and Simon (1983) tested their model on a new telephone banking system introduced by five banks located in different metropolitan areas. Their application is documented in Chapter 5.

It was stated earlier that Lilien et al. (1981), in their repeat-purchase model, considered the coefficient of external influence as a function of promotional efforts. More specifically, they represented $a(t) = a_1 d(t) + a_2 d^2(t)$, where $d(t)$ is the level of promotional expenses. Lilien et al. have demonstrated the application of their model in a study of the impact of detailing on the acceptance of ethical drugs by physicians.

For most innovations, the assumption that an innovation does not change over time is tenuous. On the contrary, because of new technical advances, competition, and reactions from adopters about their actual usage experiences, an innovation is expected to change over its life cycle. Consequently, the impact of word-of-mouth communication on potential adopters, for example, may be dependent upon the stage in the diffusion process in which it occurs.

Consider, for example, the interaction term $bN(t)(\overline{N} - N(t))$ in the internal-influence or the mixed-influence diffusion models in Chapter 2. Because

$$N(t) = \sum_{j=1}^{t} (N(j) - N(j-1)) = \sum_{j=1}^{t} n(j)$$

where $n(j)$ is number of adopters adopting the innovation at time j. Then,

$$bN(t)(\overline{N} - N(t)) = b(n(1) + n(2) --- + n(t))(\overline{N} - N(t))$$

Hence the basic diffusion models assume that the impact of word-of-mouth communication at any time t on the number of potential adopters, $(\overline{N} - N(t))$, does not depend upon when an adopter adopted the innovation. In other words, the impact of interaction between $n(1)(\overline{N} - N(t))$ and $n(t)(\overline{N} - N(t))$ is assumed to be the same. That is, b is considered constant. Although some of the flexible innovation diffusion models discussed in Chapter 3 consider the coefficient of internal influence to vary over time, they too do not distinguish its impact by stage in the diffusion process.

One approach to incorporating changes in technology and systematically varying the impact of word-of-mouth communication across adopters has been suggested by Kalish and Lilien (1983). They proposed that the interaction term in the mixed-influence diffusion model be written as follows:

$$\sum_{j=1}^{t} w_j n(j)(\overline{N} - N(j))$$

where

$$w_j = b \cdot \theta(j) \cdot \frac{1}{(1 + r)^{t-j}}$$

Here, $\theta(j)$ represents "perceived innovation quality" at time j and the parameter r reflects the intensity of influence of adopters at time j on potential adopters at time t. (Kalish and Lilien [1983] termed r a forgetting parameter.) If $r = 0$ and $\theta(j)$ is constant, the model generates a constant impact interaction term. Kalish and Lilien have applied their model in evaluating the construction of home demonstration photovoltaic programs sponsored by the Department of Energy.

## Comment

This chapter has briefly reviewed selected attempts to relax the seven major assumptions of the basic diffusion models set forth in Chapter 2. Although this review is by no means comprehensive, there clearly is a woeful lack of research on the relaxation of these assumptions. The objective here has been to elucidate key issues involved and highlight representative efforts that have been made to resolve these issues. The next chapter presents illustrative applications of the diffusion models presented in Chapters 2 through 4.

## 5. ILLUSTRATIVE APPLICATIONS

The purpose of this chapter is to illustrate specific applications of diffusion models. The five applications here collectively illustrate the types of data that have been used in modeling diffusion patterns, the variety of models that have been employed, the diversity of phenomena and innovations that have been investigated, and the different purposes to which diffusion models have been put.

### Diffusion of CAT Scanners

One of the standard applications of diffusion models is in describing (and predicting) the diffusion of an innovation through the analysis of historical data. This type of application is illustrated here for two

**TABLE 5.1**
**Summary of Results for CAT Scanners**

| Innovation | NSRL Model Parameters | | | Mean Absolute Deviation | Point of Inflection |
|---|---|---|---|---|---|
| | $b$ | $\bar{F}$ | $\delta$ | | |
| CAT head scanner | 0.9645 | 0.56 | 0.6644 | 2.78 | 0.40 |
| CAT body scanner | 1.3996 | 0.47 | 0.7899 | 1.75 | 0.44 |

NOTE: Abstracted from Easingwood et al. (1981).

medical innovations—CAT head scanners and CAT body scanners—analyzed by Easingwood et al. (1981) by means of the NSRL model discussed in Chapter 3. The data, however, are not from a census. They were collected from a survey of 206 hositals throughout the United States.[24] Surveyed hospitals were asked to identify themselves as adopters or nonadopters of each type of scanner. If adopters, they were requested to provide the date(s) of adoption. The survey indicated that by 1978, of the 206 hospitals, 113 hospitals (54.85%) had adopted the CAT head scanner and 97 had adopted the CAT body scanner. Actual adoption data are shown below:

| Year | Number of Adopters Per Year | |
|---|---|---|
| | CAT Head Scanner | CAT Body Scanner |
| 1972 | 1 | — |
| 1973 | 4 | 1 |
| 1974 | 10 | 1 |
| 1975 | 34 | 9 |
| 1976 | 33 | 30 |
| 1977 | 26 | 39 |
| 1978 | 5 | 17 |
| | 113 | 97 |

These data were used to calibrate the NSRL model through a nonlinear regression analysis algorithm by means of the following discrete analog:

$$F(t + 1) - F(t) = bF(t)^{\delta}(\bar{F} - F(t))$$

Note that the specification assumes $F \neq 1$. Table 5.1 presents a summary of the results; Figures 5.1 and 5.2 depict actual versus fitted values for

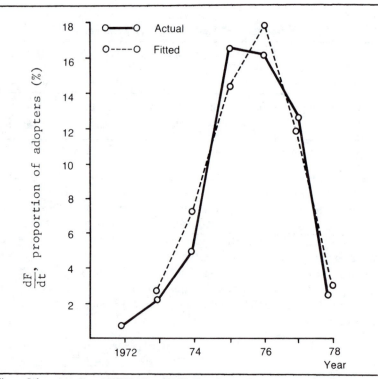

**Figure 5.1**    Actual and NSRL Fitted Diffusion Curves for CAT Head Scanners

the two innovations. Figure 5.3 depicts the time-varying value of the coefficient of internal-influence for the two innovations. Perhaps the most interesting result in Table 5.1 is the value of $\delta$ and the point of inflection. For both innovations the value of $\delta$ is less than one and the maximum adoption occurred around 40% penetration. Consistent with the NSRL model calculus, the results clearly indicate that these innovations were adopted rapidly by the hospitals surveyed and the impact of internal-influence (word-of-mouth) declined with time. It is interesting to note that these results support Rogers's (1983: 237) case analysis of CAT scanners. He has characterized CAT scanners as an illustration of over-adoption or a case of "technology run wild."

This application represents the use of a flexible diffusion model to describe a diffusion pattern by means of historical data. It also illustrates the time-varing nature of the word-of-mouth effect.

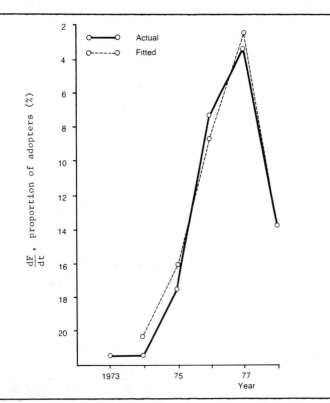

**Figure 5.2**  Actual and NSRL Fitted Diffusion Curves for CAT Body Scanners

## Diffusion of Longwall Mining Technologies

Application of diffusion models presented in Chapter 2 requires the estimation of the upper limit or ceiling $\bar{N}$ to model the diffusion pattern. An interesting approach to estimating the ceiling and the diffusion pattern that combines historical data and expert opinions and user value judgments has been suggested by Souder and Quaddus (1982). They first express the fundamental diffusion model, equation 1, as

$$\frac{dF(t)}{dt} = g(t)(\bar{F} - F(t)) \qquad [27]$$

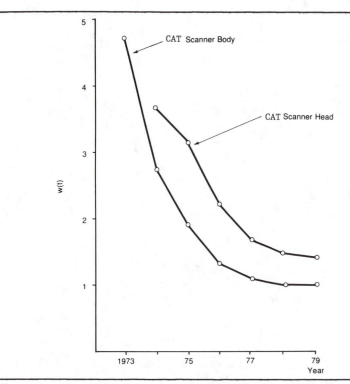

**Figure 5.3** Time-Varying Values of the Coefficient of Internal-Influence for CAT Scanners

where

$$g(t) = c_1 + c_2 t + c_3 t^2 \tag{28}$$

and $F(t) = N(t)/M$ and $\overline{F} = \overline{N}/M$, M being the population of the social system. Substitution of equation 28 into equation 27 and simple integration yields

$$\ln\left(\frac{1}{\overline{F} - F(t)}\right) = c_1 t + \frac{c_2 t^2}{2} + \frac{c_3 t^3}{3} + c$$

where c is a constant of integration. Letting

$$a_1 = c, a_2 = c_1, a_3 = \frac{c_2}{2} \text{ and } a_4 = \frac{c_3}{3}$$

the model becomes

$$\ln\left(\frac{1}{\overline{F} - F(t)}\right) = a_1 + a_2 t + a_3 t^2 + a_4 t^3 \qquad [29]$$

Before using equation 29 on the historical data to estimate parameters $a_1$, $a_2$, $a_3$ and $a_4$, the ceiling $\overline{F}$ needs to be estimated. Souder and Quaddus suggested that the ceiling should depend upon the relative advantage of the innovation over its substitutes or the survival factor S. That is, $F = f(S)$ where

$$S = \frac{V(t_n) - V(t_0)}{V(t_0)} \qquad [30]$$

with $V(t_0)$ and $V(t_n)$ representing the perceived value or subjective worth of an innovation at time $t_0$ and time $t_n$ (the terminal value of V) where $t_n \gg t_0$. More specifically, they suggest that

$$\frac{d\overline{F}(S)}{dS} = Ke^{-S} \qquad [31]$$

where K is a constant. Assuming $\overline{F}(S) = 1.0$ when $S = \infty$ and $\overline{F}(S) = F(t_0) = .01$ (1%) when $S = 0$, simple integration of equation 31 yields the following:

$$\overline{F}(S) = 1 - 0.99 \, e^{-S} \qquad [32]$$

Hence, for a particular innovation, if $V(t_0)$ and $V(t_n)$ can be derived from expert opinions or user value judgments, S can be determined from equation 30, $\overline{F}$ can be determined from equation 32 and, consequently, historical data can be used to estimate the diffusion equation 29.

To estimate $V(t_n)$ and $V(t_o)$, Souder and Quaddus (1982) suggested the use of linear scoring models, for example:

$$V_i = \frac{L_i}{\sum\limits_{k=1}^{I} L_k}$$

and

$$L_i = \sum\limits_{j=1}^{J} w_j S_{ij}$$

That is, for times $t_o$ and $t_n$, experts and users are asked to evaluate each of I innovations on J attributes by assigning a score $S_{ij}$, with the relative importance of the attribute given by $w_j$.

Souder and Quaddus have demonstrated their approach in an assessment of the diffusion of longwall mining technology with respect to three other competing underground mining technologies currently being replaced by the longwall technology. A group of actual and potential longwall users, equipment manufacturers, mining engineers, and mining research personnel were asked to formulate the attributes, identify the relative importance of these attributes, and evaluate the four technologies on these attributes for the years 1950 (when $t = t_0$ and $F(t_0) = .01$) and 2000, the terminal year when current longwall technology is expected to have its maximum possible technological development. Based on the judgmental data of these individuals on eight attributes (productivity, health and safety, percentage recovery, investment, depth of cover, roof support, cutting rate, and conveying rate), Souder and Quaddus obtained a value of $V(t_n) = 0.379$ and $V(t_0) = .148$ with $S = 1.56$ and $\overline{F} = 0.79$ for the longwall technology. Substituting the value of $\overline{F}$ in equation 29 and using available historical data on the adoption of longwall technology, they estimated the following diffusion model by means of ordinary least squares:

$$\ln\left(\frac{1}{0.79 - F(t)}\right) = 0.2336 + .0078t - .00068t^2 + .000019t^3$$

with $R^2 = .985$. From this equation, they forecast $\overline{F} = 0.54$ (54%) for the peak year 2000. Of course, only time can verify the accuracy of their prediction.

This application represents the integrated use of both historical data and expert opinions to forecast the diffusion pattern of an innovation. In addition, it presents an approach for determining the ceiling on the number of potential adopters of an innovation. Finally, it illustrates an application of the fundamental diffusion model in which the coefficient of diffusion, $g(t)$, is expressed as a function of time rather than the number of previous adopters.

## Diffusion of Oral Contraceptives (The Pill) in Thailand

This application, by Sharif and Ramanathan (1981), illustrates the application of dynamic potential adopter diffusion models. Sharif and Ramanathan considered the integration of four models of the potential adopter population with the three different diffusion models. The three diffusion models are as follows:

*Model 1:* $\quad \dfrac{dN(t)}{dt} = a(\bar{N}(t) - N(t))$

*Model 2:* $\quad \dfrac{dN(t)}{dt} = \dfrac{b}{\bar{N}(t)} (\bar{N}(t) - N(t)) N(t)$

*Model 3:* $\quad \dfrac{dN(t)}{dt} = a(\bar{N}(t) - N(t)) + \dfrac{b}{\bar{N}(t)} (\bar{N}(t) - N(t)) N(t)$

and

$$N(t = t_0) = N_0$$

Model 1 is an external-influence diffusion model; Models 2 and 3 are internal-influence and mixed-influence diffusion models, respectively.

For each of these models, Sharif and Ramanathan formulated the following four models to represent the potential adopter population:

$\bar{N}(t) = \bar{N}_0 e^{gt}$, where $\bar{N}_0 > 0$, $g > 0$

$\bar{N}(t) = \bar{N}_0 (1 + \alpha t)$, where $\bar{N}_0 > 0$, $\alpha > 0$

$$\bar{N}(t) = \frac{\kappa}{1 + \mu e^{-\lambda t}} \text{, where } \kappa > 0, \mu > 0, \lambda > 0$$

$$\bar{N}(t) = \kappa - ke^{-\theta t}, \text{ where } \kappa > 0, k > 0, \theta > 0$$

where $\bar{N}_0$ is the market potential at $t = t_0$ and g, $\alpha$, $\kappa$, $\mu$, $\lambda$, k, and $\theta$ are constants

Substitution of the potential adopter population models into the three diffusion models and further integration, as indicated by Shariff and Ramanathan, reveals that exact solutions amenable to regression analysis are obtainable for the following cases:

*Model 1:* (a) $\bar{N}(t) = \bar{N}_0 e^{gt}$

(b) $\bar{N}(t) = \bar{N}_0(1 + \alpha t)$

(c) $\bar{N}(t) = \kappa - ke^{-\theta t}$

*Model 2:* (a) $\bar{N}(t) = \bar{N}_0 e^{gt}$

(b) $\bar{N}(t) = \dfrac{\kappa}{1 + \mu e^{-\lambda t}}$

*Model 3:* (a) $\bar{N}(t) = \bar{N}_0 e^{gt}$

Exact solutions for each of these cases are given below.

*Model 1:* (a) $N(t) = \left( N_0 - \dfrac{a\bar{N}_0}{a + g} \right) e^{-at} + \dfrac{a\bar{N}_0}{a + g} e^{gt}$     [33]

$$N_0 \leqslant \bar{N}(t = 0) = \bar{N}_0, N_0 \geqslant 0$$

(b) $N(t) = \left( N_0 - \bar{N}_0 \left( \dfrac{a - \alpha}{a} \right) \right) e^{-at}$

$$+ \bar{N}_0(1 + \alpha t) - \dfrac{\alpha \bar{N}_0}{a} \qquad [34]$$

$$N_0 \leqslant \bar{N}(t = 0) = \bar{N}_0, \ N_0 \geqslant 0, \ a > \alpha$$

(c) $\quad N(t) = \left( \dfrac{ak}{a - \theta} - (\kappa - N_0) \right) e^{-at} + \kappa - \dfrac{ak}{a - \theta} e^{-\theta t}$ [35]

$$N_0 \leqslant \bar{N}(t = 0) = \kappa - k, \ N_0 \geqslant 0, \ a > \theta$$

*Model 2:* (a) $\quad N(t) = \dfrac{\bar{N}_0 e^{gt}}{\left( \dfrac{\bar{N}_0}{N_0} - \dfrac{b}{b - g} \right) e^{(b-g)t} + \dfrac{b}{b - g}}$ [36]

$$N_0 \leqslant \bar{N}(t = 0) = \bar{N}_0, \ N_0 > 0, \ b > g$$

(b) $\quad N(t) = \dfrac{\kappa}{1 + \left( \left( \dfrac{\kappa}{N_0} - 1 \right) - \dfrac{b\mu}{b - \lambda} \right) e^{-bt} + \dfrac{b\mu}{b - \lambda} e^{-\lambda t}}$ [37]

$$N_0 \leqslant \bar{N}(t = 0) = \dfrac{\kappa}{1 + \mu}, \ N_0 > 0, \ b > \lambda$$

*Model 3:* (a) $\quad N(t) = \bar{N}_0 e^{gt} \left( \dfrac{\left( \dfrac{\phi_1 - \phi_2}{2} \right) - \phi_3 \left( \dfrac{\phi_1 + \phi_2}{2} \right) e^{-\phi_1 t}}{b + b \, \phi_3 e^{-\phi_1 t}} \right)$ [38]

where

$$\phi_1 = \sqrt{(g + a - b)^2 + 4a \, b}$$

$$\phi_2 = (g + a - b)$$

$$\phi_3 = \dfrac{\left( \dfrac{\phi_1 - \phi_2}{2} \right) - \dfrac{bN_0}{\bar{N}_0}}{\left( \dfrac{\phi_1 + \phi_2}{2} \right) + \dfrac{bN_0}{\bar{N}_0}}$$

$$N_0 \leqslant \bar{N}(t = 0) = \bar{N}_0, \ N_0 > 0$$

Sharif and Ramanathan applied these models in the following situations: diffusion of flouridated water usage in the United States, diffusion of credit card banking in the United States, diffusion of oral contraceptives in Thailand, and diffusion of tractors in Thailand. Their approach involved using nonlinear estimation procedures on equations 33 through 38 and selecting that model equation yielding the minimum residual sum of squares. Table 5.2 summarizes their results for the diffusion of oral contraceptives in Thailand. Model 2(b), equation 37, gives the best fit. Note that this is a significant improvement over the fits for the models that assume $\overline{N}$ is constant (see Table 5.2).

This application represents the use of diffusion models when dynamic potential adopter populations exist. Moreover, it illustrates the use of alternative diffusion model formulations to best describe a given diffusion pattern.

### Diffusion of Computer Terminals in an Established Engineering Environment

As previously discussed, the seminal work in developing empirical models of the process by which a new product or technology substitutes for an established product or technology in a firm is due to Mansfield (1961). Using the pure internal-influence model, Mansfield attempted to establish empirical support for his model in four disparate industrial sectors—railroads, coal, steel, and breweries. By assuming that the coefficient of internal-influence is affected by factors related to the industry and the innovation, he was able to establish the following regression equation:

$$b = z + 0.530\pi - 0.027I$$

where z is a constant representative of a given industry, $\pi$ is a profitability index, and I is an investment index. In the absence of historical data, a diffusion curve for an innovation can be developed by estimating z, $\pi$, and I, and hence, b. Although examples of Mansfield's approach can be found in Blackman (1974), it is illustrated here for the diffusion of an innovation among individuals (rather than firms). This illustration is due to Randles (1983).

Randles has applied the Mansfield model to the diffusion of computer terminals among workers in the aerospace division of a company. Because he assumed that the terminals would be replacing two generations of hand calculators used by the workers, Randles first used the

**TABLE 5.2**
**Results of Nonlinear Regression Analysis for the Diffusion**
**of Oral Contraceptives in Thailand**

| Model | Parameter Values | Residual Sum of Squares |
|-------|------------------|-------------------------|
| Model 2<br>$\overline{N}(t) = \overline{N}$ (constant) | $b = 1.0795$<br>$\overline{N} = 2120.80$ | 234,773.00 |
| Model 2 (a)<br>$\overline{N}(t) = \overline{N}_0 e^{gt}$ | $b = 1.6650$<br>$\overline{N}_0 = 455.47$<br>$g = 0.2098$ | 1,185.84 |
| Model 2 (b)<br>$\overline{N}(t) = \dfrac{\kappa}{1 + \mu e^{-\lambda t}}$ | $b = 1.7321$<br>$\kappa = 6480.30$<br>$\mu = 7.7857$<br>$\lambda = 0.2818$ | 578.98 |
| Model 3<br>$\overline{N}(t) = \overline{N}$ (constant) | $a = 2.8787 \times 10^{-2}$<br>$b = 0.4088$<br>$\overline{N} = 3036.54$ | 15,551.20 |
| Model 3 (a)<br>$\overline{N}(t) = \overline{N}_0 e^{gt}$ | $a = 1.9412 \times 10^{-2}$<br>$b = 1.4320$<br>$\overline{N}_0 = 486.5$<br>$g = 0.2033$ | 6,602.60 |

NOTE: Abstracted from Sharif and Ramanathan (1981).

following model to develop diffusion curves for the adoption of two generations of hand calculators:

$$\frac{dF(t)}{dt} = bF(t)(\overline{F} - F(t)) \text{ and } F(t = t_0) = F_0$$

or

$$\ln\left(\frac{F(t)}{\overline{F} - F(t)}\right) = c + bt \qquad [39]$$

where

$$c = \ln\left(\frac{F_0}{\overline{F} - F_0}\right) - bt_0 = \text{constant}$$

Also,

$$F(t) = \frac{\overline{F}}{1 + \exp(-(c + bt))} \qquad [40]$$

Using equation 39 and survey data on the adoption of hand calculators, regression analysis was used to develop two sets of estimates. For the initial diffusion of hand calculators

c = -6.650781, b = 0.640703, $\overline{F}$ = 0.955, $R^2$ = 0.98.

For the second generation diffusion,

c = 15.552417, b = 1.033016, $\overline{F}$ = 0.918, $R^2$ = 0.98.

To use equation 40 for the diffusion of computer terminals, it is first necessary to estimate $\overline{F}$, c, and b. Randles used two approaches to estimate b. One approach involved using limited historical data (3 data points) available on the adoption of computer terminals in the organization. Least squares analysis of equation 39 provided the value of b = 0.540815. The other approach consisted of applying Mansfield's formulation of hand calculator data, that is,

$$b = z + b_1\pi + b_2I \qquad [41]$$

However, because only two data points were available (on the values of b), certain assumptions were made to reduce equation 41 to a two parameter equation. First, Randles assumed that the profit factor or motivation was the same for all employees. That is, $K = z + b_1\pi$ = constant. Second, for the terminal use, because the corporation made the monetary investment, it was assumed that the only investment from employees was time investment. Consequently, equation 41 was rewritten as

$$b = K + UI \qquad [42]$$

where K and U are constants.

Then, in order to estimate K and U, the following values of I were specified for the two generations of hand calculators:

$$I_1 = \frac{C_1}{Rate} + h = 8 + h \qquad [43]$$

$$I_2 = \frac{C_2}{\text{Rate}} + 0.65h = 5.22 + 0.65h \qquad [44]$$

where $C_1$ = average cost of first generation calculators = \$112.47; $C_2$ = average cost of second generation calculators = \$73.06; Rate = average hourly rate paid in the organization = \$14/hour; and h = hours to obtain nominal proficiency. The value of 0.65 in equation 44 represents an estimate of learning for similar repetitive engineering tasks. Because b = 0.640703 for the first generation of hand calculators and b = 1.033016 for the second generation, constants K and U were easily calculated in terms of h by means of equations 43 and 44. Furthermore, assuming H = $\alpha$h, where H is the hours required to obtain nominal proficiency on a terminal and $\alpha$ is a constant, the following expression was established for the coefficient of internal-influence for the terminals:

$$b = 0.640703 + 0.392313 \left( \frac{8 + (1 - \alpha)h}{2.78 + 0.35h} \right) \qquad [45]$$

Table 5.3 reproduces values of b for various intuitive values of $\alpha$ and h. Given these values and the value of b = 0.540815 for the limited data on computer terminals, a final value of b = 0.540 was selected to use in equation 40 for the diffusion of computer terminals.

Given the values of $\overline{F}$ = .955 and .918 for the two generations of hand calculators, respectively, an exponential relationship was assumed for $\overline{F}$ for computer terminals. That is, because $\overline{F}$ (second generation calculators) = $(.955)^2$ = .918, hence $\overline{F}$ (terminals) = $(.918)^2$ = .842. This value was inserted into equation 40 such that the final model was as follows:

$$F(t) = \frac{.842}{1 + \exp(-(c + .540t))} \qquad [46]$$

After calculating the value of c by considering the actual number of adoptions for the third data point, Randles used equation 46 to project a diffusion curve for computer terminals in the organization.

This application illustrates three aspects of diffusion curve modeling. First, it shows how explanatory variables can be incorporated into a diffusion model. Second, it shows how parameter estimates of analogous innovations to the one being investigated can be used to develop param-

**TABLE 5.3**
**Values of b for Diffusion of Terminals**

| Alpha | Hours | | | | | |
|-------|-------|-------|-------|-------|-------|-------|
| | 8.0 | 10.0 | 12.0 | 14.0 | 16.0 | 18.0 |
| 1.55 | 0.893808 | 0.796878 | 0.719390 | 0.656028 | 0.603251 | 0.558611 |
| 1.65 | 0.837563 | 0.734409 | 0.651944 | 0.584513 | 0.528346 | 0.480840 |
| 1.70 | 0.809440 | 0.703173 | 0.618221 | 0.548755 | 0.490894 | 0.441954 |
| 1.80 | 0.753194 | 0.640703 | 0.550774 | 0.477239 | 0.415989 | 0.364183 |
| 2.00 | 0.640703 | 0.515763 | 0.415882 | 0.334208 | 0.266180 | 0.208640 |
| 2.20 | 0.528212 | 0.390822 | 0.280989 | 0.191178 | 0.116371 | 0.053098 |

SOURCE: Randles (1983).

eter estimates for the innovation. Third, it again shows the creative application of a diffusion model in the presence of limited data.

### Diffusion of Telephone-Based Banking Services

The final application included in this section illustrates the incorporation of marketing mix variables into a fundamental diffusion model. More specifically, the application incorporates advertising into the mixed-influence diffusion model.

As discussed in Chapter 4, Horsky and Simon (1983) hypothesized that advertising serves to inform innovators of the existence and value of an innovation and hence its effect should be incorporated into the coefficient of external-influence. They specified the following model to test this hypothesis:

$$\frac{dN(t)}{dt} = (a_1 + a_2 \ln A(t) + bN(t))(\bar{N} - N(t))$$

The discrete analog of this model is amenable to estimation by ordinary least squares and can be written as

$$N(t+1) - N(t) = a_1(\bar{N} - N(t)) + a_2 \ln A(t)(\bar{N} - N(t))$$

$$+ bN(t)(\bar{N} - N(t)).$$

**TABLE 5.4**
**Estimates of Diffusion Model Parameters**

| SMSA | Market Potential $\overline{N}$ | Promotional Effects | | Word of Mouth $(b \cdot 10^{+5})$ | Goodness of Fit $(R^2)$ | Number of Monthly Observations* |
|------|------|------|------|------|------|------|
| | | Publicity $(a_1 \cdot 10^{+3})$ | Advertising $(a_2 \cdot 10^{+3})$ | | | |
| A | 1,700 | 1.52 (4.1)** | 2.99 (1.77) | 3.64 (1.29) | 0.66 | 14 |
| B | 3,600 | 0.64 (0.17) | 1.32 (0.35) | 2.08 (0.32) | 0.91 | 16 |
| C | 6,200 | 0.57 (0.19) | 0.89 (0.21) | 1.28 (0.61) | 0.82 | 20 |
| D | 21,500 | 1.53 (0.70) | 0.23 (0.10) | 0.40 (0.11) | 0.74 | 21 |
| E | 22,800 | 1.17 (0.43) | 0.15 (0.04) | 0.29 (0.07) | 0.82 | 13 |

NOTE: Abstracted from Horsky and Simon (1983).
*This is frequently less than the period for which the bank has been offering the service due to elimination of observations in which expanded services (modified products) were offered.
**Values in parentheses are standard errors.

To illustrate the application of their model, Horsky and Simon (1983) analyzed the diffusion of a telephone banking service in five different Standard Metropolitan Statistical Areas (SMSAs) ranging from the East coast to the Midwest. This service, which was introduced by mutual savings banks between October 1974 and April 1975, permits consumers to pay bills via telephone by first opening a checking or savings account and then providing the institution with the names and personal account numbers of all the merchants to whom they wish to pay bills. The number of adoptions was measured by the number of newly opened accounts; advertising outlays represented the total expenditures on advertising in media, direct mail, and point-of-sale material.

Table 5.4 presents the results of the discrete diffusion model developed by Horsky and Simon. Because they considered the ceiling $\overline{N}$ as a model parameter, to estimate $a_1$, $a_2$, $b$, and $\overline{N}$ they varied the values of $\overline{N}$ to obtain the highest $R^2$. As indicated by the $R^2$ values, their model performed relatively well for the different SMSAs. Given the values of the coefficients in Table 5.4, the contribution of the various diffusion model components (advertising and word-of-mouth) on period-by-period adoptions can be calculated.

This application illustrates how marketing mix variables can be explicitly incorporated into a diffusion model so that their influence on model parameters and, ultimately, the diffusion pattern, can be directly examined and evaluated.

## Comment

This chapter briefly reviewed five illustrative applications of diffusion models. Collectively these applications provide creative insights and ideas regarding the utility of diffusion models in a variety of contexts. Even though the nature of specific applications will vary across disciplines and innovations, the models and procedures described in this and preceding chapters should prove useful in modeling any temporal diffusion pattern.

## 6. STATUS AND OUTLOOK

Although the diffusion models discussed in the previous sections may at times appear either superficial and/or simplistic, in fact they represent a powerful class of conceptual tools. As illustrated here, they have been applied to a broad range of diffusion-based phenomena across a multitude of disciplines.

In spite of diverse applications, careful review of the literature reveals that, in general, diffusion models have been put to three distinct uses. Initially, they were used to *describe* behavioral events such as the spread of rumors or the diffusion of certain innovations. As such, they were used in an explanatory mode and at times applied when testing specific diffusion-based hypotheses. The latter is illustrated by the work of Mansfield (1961), who used diffusion curves to test hypotheses about the evolution of technology.

A second use has been *normative*. Specifically, diffusion models have often been viewed as normative models. In this context, for example, marketers have used diffusion models as the basis of how a product should be marketed, given the ("natural") shape of the diffusion (sales growth) curve. As an aside, virtually all applications of diffusion models are normative in nature, because the researchers are assuming that, either explicitly or implicitly, there should be certain observed regularities in the data being analyzed. Indeed, if such an assumption were not made, there would be no need for diffusion models.[25]

A third and perhaps most common use has been in *forecasting*. This is most prevalent in the business area, where attempts have been made to forecast the success or failure of new products. In this context, diffusion models are but one alternative approach to forecasting. Although they have been used extensively in technological forecasting applications (Martino, 1983), their value in forecasting traditional time-series data has yet to be fully established. When considering temporal diffusion models for forecasting applications, it is first necessary to evaluate their characteristics and capabilities relative to alternative forecasting techniques. For example, consider the simplified comparison of temporal diffusion models and the Box-Jenkins approach (e.g., Makridakis et al., 1983) to forecasting presented in Table 6.1. If one were making a choice as to which forecasting approach to employ, these are the types of comparisons required in selecting the most appropriate approach.

Although diffusion models have existed in one form or another for several decades, only recently have they been rigorously examined and their properties investigated. Even so, much remains to be done from both a practical as well as a theoretical perspective. In the area of forecasting, for instance, there is a virtual paucity of research on the validity of forecasts derived using diffusion models, Validations that have been carried out have only employed a one-step-ahead approach. There is a need to empirically compare the forecasting capabilities of diffusion models with other time-series techniques (e.g., the Box-Jenkins approach). Eventually, diffusion models will likely be combined with other forecasting techniques. For instance, by combining diffusion models with conjoint analysis-based simulators (Green and Wind, 1975) it may be possible to accurately forecast new product sales prior to the product actually being introduced into the marketplace.

Moreover, from both a theoretical and a practical perspective it is necessary to study what variables should be included in diffusion models and what form these models should take. For example, in business applications the efficacy of including a price and/or advertising variable needs to be investigated as well as determining the form in which it or they should be included. Likewise, there is a need to incorporate "rescinded adoptions" into a diffusion model and, in some instances, "repeat adoptions" or "replacement adoptions."

Briefly, there still remains a considerable amount of work on diffusion models. In addition to developing even more extensions or refinements of currently existing deterministic models, there is a need to

**TABLE 6.1**
**Simplified Comparison of Diffusion and Box-Jenkins**
**Approaches to Forecasting**

| Diffusion Model Characteristics | Box-Jenkins Characteristics |
|---|---|
| Theory-based | Data-driven (atheoretic) |
| Short-term forecasting (2-3 periods) | Short-term forecasting (2-3 periods) |
| Few data points required to estimate parameters | Relatively many data points required to estimate parameters |
| Parameter estimation is easy | Sophisticated parameter estimation procedure required |
| Application is relatively straightforward | Application requires extensive judgment |
| Descriptive and normative applications | Descriptive applications only |
| Ignores idiosyncrasies of time-series data (e.g., auto correlations) | Specifically designed for time-series data |

NOTE: Adapted from Mahajan and Wind (1985).

incorporate stochastic elements into diffusion models to increase their realism and relevancy (e.g., Tapiero, 1983). In fact, there is an urgent need for a unified theory of diffusion models. Only by so doing will it be possible to model certain behavioral phenomena without making unrealistic assumptions or simplifications.

Simultaneously, there is a need to apply diffusion models to what currently may be thought of as nontraditional data. For example, Monin et al. (1976) have already suggested that diffusion models might be applied when analyzing changes in attitudes since, they argue, there is a definite evolution of attitudes that lends itself to a diffusion-like analytical approach. More recently, Becker and Speltz (1983) have attempted to apply diffusion curve concepts when examining research and development productivity. Although there is presently not enough evidence to judge the efficacy of these and similar applications, they suggest the possibility that diffusion models can be used in much broader contexts than they traditionally have been.

Although considerable work has been done on diffusion models, it may well be that researchers are on the verge of identifying not only new applications, but new and even more useful models for studying phenomena of both a behavioral and technical nature, phenomena that heretofore may have not been perceived as amenable to any systematic analysis. Therefore, it is with optimism that researchers should approach diffusion models as they continue to build a better, more salient set of models for application to a broad range of phenomena.

# APPENDIX
## DERIVATION OF VON BERTALANFFY'S MODEL

Using the notation of Chapter 2, the Von Bertalanffy model can be written as

$$\frac{dN(t)}{dt} = \frac{b}{1-\theta} N^{\theta}(t) (\bar{N}^{1-\theta} - N^{1-\theta}(t)) \qquad [A-1]$$

Assuming $N(t = t_0) = N_0$, integration of A-1 yields

$$N(t) = [\bar{N}^{1-\theta} - (\bar{N}^{1-\theta} - N_0^{1-\theta}) \exp(-b(t-t_0))]^{\frac{1}{1-\theta}} \qquad [A-2]$$

Note that when $\theta = 0$ and $N(t = t_0 = 0) = 0$, equations A-1 and A-2 reduce to:

$$\frac{dN(t)}{dt} = b(\bar{N} - N(t)) \quad \text{and} \quad N(t) = \bar{N}(1 - \exp(-bt))$$

which is the external-influence model presented in Chapter 2 with $b = a$. On the other hand, if $\theta = 2$, equations A-1 and A-2 become:

$$\frac{dN(t)}{dt} = \frac{b}{\bar{N}}(\bar{N} - N(t)) N(t)$$

$$N(t) = \frac{\bar{N}}{1 + \frac{(\bar{N} - N_0)}{N_0} \exp(-b(t-t_0))}$$

which is the internal-influence model presented in Chapter 2 with the coefficient of internal influence scaled by $\bar{N}$.

The Von Bertalanffy model is not defined at $\theta = 1$. However, as $\theta \to 1$, the model reduces to the Gompertz diffusion model. This can be easily shown by rewriting equation A-1:

$$\frac{dN(t)}{dt} = bN(t)\left[\frac{1}{1-\theta}\left(\left(\frac{\bar{N}}{N(t)}\right)^{1-\theta} - 1\right)\right] \qquad [A-3]$$

As $\theta \to 1$, the limiting value of

$$\frac{1}{(1-\theta)}\left(\left(\frac{\bar{N}}{N(t)}\right)^{1-\theta} - 1\right)$$

is $\ln(\bar{N}/N(t))$. In order to show this, let $\bar{N}/N(t) = p$ and $1 - \theta = x$. Using L'Hospital's Rule,

$$\lim_{x \to 0} \frac{p^x - 1}{x} = \lim_{x \to 0} \frac{\frac{d}{dx}(p^x - 1)}{dx/dx} = \lim_{x \to 0} p^x \ln p = \ln p$$

Hence, equation A-3 reduces to

$$\frac{dN(t)}{dt} = bN(t)(\ln\bar{N} - \ln N(t))$$

which is the Gompertz model. Hence, the Von Bertalanffy model subsumes the external-influence model as well as the logistic and Gompertz forms of the internal-influence model.

Defining $F(t) = N(t)/\bar{N}$, the fraction of potential adopters who adopt the innovation by time t, equation A-1 can be restated as follows:

$$\frac{dF(t)}{dt} = \frac{b}{1-\theta} F^\theta(1 - F^{1-\theta}) \qquad [A-4]$$

### Point of Inflection

The Von Bertalanffy model possesses a flexible point of inflection, $F^*$. In fact, $F^* \to 0$ as $\theta \to 0$, $F^* \to 1$ as $\theta \to \infty$, and $F^* \to 1/e$ as $\theta \to 1$. These results can be shown by first deriving the point of inflection for the model. The point of inflection for the Von Bertalanffy model can be obtained by differentiating equation A-4 with respect to F, equating it to zero and solving for F*. Differentiation of equation A-4 and further simplification yields:

$$F^* = (\theta)^{\frac{1}{1-\theta}} \qquad [A\text{-}5]$$

Note from equation A-2 that

$$F = [1 - (1 - F_0^{1-\theta}) \exp(-b(t - t_0))]^{\frac{1}{1-\theta}} \qquad [A\text{-}6]$$

Substitution of equation A-6 into equation A-5 and further simplification yields the time, t*, at which the point of inflection occurs. That is,

$$t^* = t_0 + \frac{1}{b} \ln\left(\frac{1 - F_0^{1-\theta}}{1-\theta}\right) \qquad [A\text{-}7]$$

In order to show that F* → 0 as θ → 0, let

$$z = \ln F^* = \frac{1}{1-\theta} \ln\theta.$$

Because

$$\lim_{\theta \to 0} z = \lim_{\theta \to 0} \frac{\ln\theta}{1-\theta} = -\infty,$$

hence

$$\lim_{\theta \to 0} F^* = e^{-\infty} = 0. \text{ That is, } F^* \to 0, \text{ as } \theta \to 0.$$

Similarly, when θ → ∞, using L'Hospital's Rule,

$$\lim_{\theta \to \infty} z = \lim_{\theta \to \infty} \frac{1}{1-\theta} \ln\theta = \lim_{\theta \to \infty} \frac{1/\theta}{-1} = 0$$

Hence,

$$\lim_{\theta \to \infty} F^* = e^0 = 1. \text{ That is, } F^* \to 1, \text{ as } \theta \to \infty.$$

It was shown earlier that as θ → 1, the Von Bertalanffy model reduces to the Gompertz diffusion model. It can be easily shown that as θ → 1,

$F^* = 1/e$, the point of inflection for the Gompertz model. Using L'Hospital's Rule again,

$$\lim_{\theta \to 1} z = \lim_{\theta \to 1} \frac{1}{1-\theta} \ln\theta = \lim_{\theta \to 1} \frac{1/\theta}{-1} = -1$$

Hence,

$$\lim_{\theta \to 1} F^* = e^{-1} = \frac{1}{e}$$

Also, because $dF^*/d\theta > 0$, the point of inflection for the Von Bertalanffy model can occur at any stage in the diffusion process.

### Symmetry

The fact that the Von Bertalanffy model subsumes the logistic internal-influence (which is symmetric) and the Gompertz internal-influence (which is asymmetric) models clearly illustrate that the model can accommodate both symmetric and nonsymmetric diffusion patterns.

### Maximum Diffusion Level

The maximum value of $dF(t)/dt$ for the Von Bertalanffy model is b as $\theta \to 0$ and is zero when $\theta \to \infty$. That is, the range of maximum values is 0 through b. Note that, at the point of inflection (substituting equation A-5 into equation A-4),

$$\frac{dF(t)}{dt} \bigg|_{\substack{max \\ at\ F^*}} = b(\theta)^{\frac{\theta}{1-\theta}}$$

Let

$$z = \ln \frac{1}{b} \frac{dF(t)}{dt} \bigg|_{max} = \frac{\theta}{1-\theta} \ln\theta$$

Using L'Hospital's rule,

$$\lim_{\theta \to 0} z = \lim_{\theta \to 0} \frac{\theta}{1-\theta} \ln\theta = \lim_{\theta \to 0} \frac{\ln\theta}{\frac{1}{\theta}-1}$$

$$= \lim_{\theta \to 0} \frac{1/\theta}{-1/\theta^2} = \lim_{\theta \to 0} (-\theta) = 0$$

Hence,

$$\lim_{\theta \to 0} z = \lim_{\theta \to 0} \ln \frac{1}{b} \left. \frac{dF(t)}{dt} \right|_{max} = 0$$

or

$$\left. \frac{dF}{dt} \right|_{max} = b$$

That is, as $\theta \to 0$,

$$\left. \frac{dF(t)}{dt} \right|_{max} \to b$$

Similarly,

$$\lim_{\theta \to \infty} z = \lim_{\theta \to \infty} \frac{\ln\theta}{\frac{1}{\theta} - 1} = \lim_{\theta \to \infty} \frac{1/\theta}{-1/\theta^2}$$

$$= \lim_{\theta \to \infty} (-\theta) = -\infty$$

Hence,

$$\lim_{\theta \to \infty} z = \lim_{\theta \to \infty} \ln \frac{1}{b} \left. \frac{dF(t)}{dt} \right|_{max} = -\infty$$

or

$$\left. \frac{1}{b} \frac{dF(t)}{dt} \right|_{max} = e^{-\infty} = 0$$

That is, as

$$\theta \to \infty, \left. \frac{dF(t)}{dt} \right|_{max} \to 0$$

Hence, the range of maximum values is zero through b.

# NOTES

1. See Hamblin et al. (1973) for a historical overview of these applications in sociology and communications.

2. Thus $\overline{N}$ can be considered the *ceiling* on the total number of possible adoptions or the asymptote of the diffusion curve.

3. To facilitate comparison of the various diffusion models discussed, all models will be expressed in terms of this notation and terminology.

4. Although g(t) is sometimes referred to as a "constant of proportionality," it is "constant" only when the specific characteristics of a diffusion process have been delineated.

5. Much of the discussion in this section is drawn from Mahajan and Schoeman (1977).

6. At times a has been interpreted as a coefficient of innovation. This, though, is probably too restrictive an interpretation.

7. This model has also been applied by Fourt and Woodlock (1960) in a highly cited article to forecast sales of grocery products. However, although the model "fit" the data rather well in a statistical sense, it suffered from interpretation problems due to conceptual deficiencies.

8. Note that there must be at least one initial adopter or innovator for this model to be applicable (i.e., $N_o \geq 1$), although the origin of this innovator is not specified.

9. Gray's application, however, has been criticized. See, for example, Walker (1973) and Eyestone (1977).

10. The internal-influence diffusion model can also be shown to be related to the Fisher and Pry (1971) and Blackman (1972) logistic substitution models. These models can be expressed as

$$\frac{d\,F(t)}{dt} = b'\,F(t)\,(\overline{F} - F(t))$$

where F(t) is the market share of a product or technology at time t (i.e.,

$$F(t) = \frac{N(t)}{M}$$

where M is total market size), b' is the coefficient of internal influence, and $\overline{F}$ is the market ceiling (i.e., $\overline{F} = \overline{N}/M$). In the Fisher and Pry model $\overline{F}$ is assumed to equal 1.0 (there is complete market saturation).

11. Obviously, the more time periods available the more reliable or stable parameter estimates will be. The number of time periods available, though, is in part a function of the purpose of the estimation process—predicting future adoptions or explaining a diffusion process. The former is typically undertaken at the beginning of a diffusion process when relatively few data points are available (e.g., as in sales forecasting); the latter is most often undertaken in retrospect, when more data points are available (i.e., when a diffusion

process is complete). For further discussion, see Tigert and Farivar (1981), Cyr (1983), and Meade (1984).

12. See Rogers (1983) for an extensive review of evidence regarding the existence of these stages.

13. This section is adapted from Easingwood et al. (1981, 1983).

14. Two additional models that have been used to study diffusion patterns incorporate a cumulative normal distribution function (Stapleton, 1976) or a Weibull distribution function (Pessemier, 1977; Sharif and Islam, 1980), respectively. The cumulative normal distribution yields an S-shaped curve with a fixed point of inflection occurring at $\overset{*}{F} = 0.5$. Hence, the utilization of a cumulative normal distribution to model diffusion patterns is also restrictive. Pessemier (1977) and Sharif and Islam (1980) have suggested the use of the Weibull distribution as a general model to forecast innovation diffusion. This distribution yields a nonsymmetric curve with a point of inflection that responds to the penetration pattern. Although possessing desirable diffusion curve properties, it ignores the underlying theory behind diffusion. Moreover, behavioral and managerial interpretations of the model parameters are not clear.

15. As can be noted from Table 3.1, however, the mixed-influence (Bass) model does permit some flexibility with regard to the point of inflection or timing of the maximum rate of diffusion.

16. The model derivations can be found in Sharif and Ramanathan (1981).

17. Sanatani (1981) has validated the existence of such dynamic patterns using a system dynamics simulation approach to study market penetration of new products in segmented populations.

18. Application of the fundamental mixed-influence model produced an unacceptable (negative) estimate for the b parameter.

19. These citations illustrate that, in addition to possessing the potential of providing accurate forecasts, the dynamic diffusion model has another benefit. By judicious selection of variables for S(t), it is possible to obtain explanatory insights as to *why* one innovation diffuses much more readily than another.

20. Alert readers will note the close resemblance of these equations to the classical competing population equations of Volterra and Lotka (Pielou, 1969).

21. If an innovation is introduced into more than one region (perhaps at different times), each region may be simultaneously affected by a number of different diffusion "waves."

22. An alternative approach to integrating space and time in diffusion models has been suggested by Haynes et al. (1977). Using the behavioral elements of interpersonal communication and neighborhood communication, they represented the spatial diffusion phenomenon by a second-order partial differential equation, which is analogous to the general equation used in the physical sciences to specify heat, mass and momentum transfer with an internal energy source.

23. In their model formulation, Mahajan et al. (1984) ignored the existence of neutral information.

24. See Robertson and Wind (1980) for details of the survey. For a discussion of how estimates based on data derived from a survey can be used to estimate diffusion patterns for the total social system, see Schmittlein and Mahajan (1982).

25. It is interesting to note that, although most diffusion model applications are of a normative nature, descriptive applications are the antithesis of forecasting applications. In the former application, a researcher typically has a long time series and is attempting to

describe or explain its particular shape or form. In the latter application, the researcher typically has only a very short time series (e.g., few data points) and is not interested in explaining why a pattern occurred, but in predicting what the future pattern will be. Still, these broad differences reinforce the power of diffusion models that allows them to be put to diverse uses.

# REFERENCES

BAILEY, N.T.J. (1957) Mathematical Theory of Epidemics. New York: Hafner.

BASS, F. M. (1969) "A new product growth model for consumer durables." Management Science 15: 215-227.

———(1980) "The relationship between diffusion rates, experience curves, and demand elasticities for consumer durable technological innovations." Journal of Business 53: S57-S67.

BECKER, R. H. and L. M. SPELTZ (1983) "Putting the S-Curve concept to work." Research Management 26: 31-33.

BERNHARDT, I. and K. M. MacKENZIE (1972) "Some problems in using diffusion models for new products." Management Science 19: 187-200.

BLACKMAN, A. W., Jr. (1972) "A mathematical model for trend forecasts." Technological Forecasting and Social Change 3: 441-452.

———(1974) "The market dynamics of technological substitutions." Technological Forecasting and Social Change 6: 41-63.

BRETSCHNEIDER, S. I. and V. MAHAJAN (1980) "Adaptive technological substitution models." Technological Forecasting and Social Change 18: 129-139.

BROWN, L. A. (1981) Innovation Diffusion: A New Perspective. New York: Methuen.

———and S. G. PHILLIBER (1977) "The diffusion of a population-related innovation: the planned parenthood affiliate." Social Science Quarterly 58: 215-228.

CASETTI, E. and R. K. SEMPLE (1969) "Concerning and testing of spatial diffusion hypotheses." Geographical Analysis 1: 254-259.

CHOW, G. C. (1967) "Technological change and the demand for computers." American Economic Review 57: 1117-1130.

CLARKE, D and R. J. DOLAN (1984) "A simulation analysis of alternative strategies for dynamic environments." Journal of Business 57: S179-S200.

COLEMAN, J. S., E. KATZ, and H. MENZEL (1966) Medical Innovation: A Diffusion Study. Indianapolis: Bobbs-Merrill.

CYR, A. B. (1983) "A crucial regression error in research on diffusion of state policies." Political Methodology 9: 201-214.

DIXON, R. (1980) "Hybrid corn revisited." Econometrica 48: 1451-1461.

DODSON, J. A. and E. MULLER (1978) "Models for new product diffusion through advertising and word-of-mouth." Management Science 24: 1568-1578.

DOLAN, R. J. and A. P. JEULAND (1981) "Experience curves and dynamic demand models: implications for optimal pricing strategies." Journal of Marketing 45: 52-73.

DRAPER, N. and H. SMITH (1981) Applied Regression Analysis. New York: John Wiley.

EASINGWOOD, C. J., V. MAHAJAN, and E. W. MULLER (1983) "A non-uniform influence innovation diffusion model of new product acceptance." Marketing Science 2: 273-296.

————(1981) "A nonsymmetric responding logistic model for forecasting technological substitution." Technological Forecasting and Social Change 20: 199-213.

ELIASHBERG, J. and A. P. JEULAND (1982) The Impact of Competitive Entry in a Developing Market upon Dynamic Pricing Strategies. Working paper. Philadelphia: The Wharton School, University of Pennsylvania.

EYESTONE, R. (1977) "Confusion, diffusion, and innovation." American Political Science Review 71: 441-447.

FISHER, J. C. and R. H. PRY (1971) "A simple substitution model for technological change." Technological Forecasting and Social Change 2: 75-88.

FERSHTMAN, C., V. MAHAJAN, and E. MULLER (1983) Advertising, Pricing and Stability in Oligopolistic Markets for New Products. Working paper. Dallas: Edwin L. Cox School of Business, Southern Methodist University.

FLOYD, A. (1968) "A methodology for trend forecasting of figures of merit," pp. 95-109 in J. Bright (ed.) Technological Forecasting for Industry and Government: Methods and Applications. Inglewood Cliffs, NJ: Prentice-Hall.

FOURT, L. A. and J. W. WOODLOCK (1960) "Early prediction of market success for new grocery products." Journal of Marketing 25: 31-38.

GRAY, V. (1973) "Innovation in the states: a diffusion study." The American Political Science Review 67: 1174-1182.

GREEN, P. E. and Y. WIND (1975) "New way to measure consumers' judgments." Harvard Business Review 53 (July-August): 107-117.

GRILICHES, Z. (1957) "Hybrid corn: an exploration in the economics of technological change." Econometrica 25: 501-522.

HAGERSTRAND, T. (1967) Innovation Diffusion as a Spatial Process. Chicago: University of Chicago Press.

HAMBLIN, R. L., R. B. JACOBSEN, and J.L.L. MILLER (1973) A Mathematical Theory of Social Change. New York: John Wiley.

HAYNES, K. E., V. MAHAJAN, and G. M. WHITE (1977) "Innovation diffusion: a deterministic model of space-time integration with physical analog." Social-Economic Planning Sciences 11 (February): 25-29.

HEELER, R. M. and T. P. HUSTAD (1980) "Problems in predicting new product growth for durables." Management Science 26: 1007-1020.

HENDRY, I. (1972) "The three parameter approach to long range forecasting." Long Range Planning 5: 40-45.

HORSKY, D. and L. S. SIMON (1983) "Advertising and the diffusion of new products." Marketing Science 2: 1-18.

JEULAND, A. (1981) Parsimonious Models of Diffusion of Innovation: Derivation and Comparisons. Working paper, marketing department. Chicago: Graduate School of Business, University of Chicago.

JORGENSON, S. (1983) "Optimal control of a diffusion model of new product acceptance with price-dependent total market potential." Optimal Control Applications and Methods 4: 269-276.

KALISH, S. (1983) "Monopolistic pricing with dynamic demand and product costs." Marketing Science 2: 135-160.

————and G. L. LILIEN (1983) A Market Entry Timing Model for New Technologies. Working paper. College Park: Pennsylvania State University.

KATZ, E., M. LEVIN, and H. HAMILTON (1963) "Traditions of research on the diffusion of innovation." American Sociological Review 28: 237-252.

KELLY, P. and M. KRANZBERG [eds.] (1978) Technological Innovation: A Critical Review of Current Knowledge. San Francisco: San Francisco Press.

LACKMAN, C. L. (1978) "Gompertz curve forecasting: a new product application." Journal of the Market Research Society 20: 45-57.

LAWRENCE, K. D. and W. H. LAWTON (1981) "Applications of Diffusion Models: Some Empirical Results," pp. 529-541 in Y. Wind et al. (eds.) New Product Forecasting. Lexington, MA: D. C. Heath.

LAWTON, S. B. and W. H. LAWTON (1979) "An autocatalytic model for the diffusion of educational innovations." Educational Administration Quarterly 15: 19-46.

LEKVALL, P. and C. WAHLBIN (1973) "A study of some assumptions underlying innovation diffusion functions." Swedish Journal of Economics 75: 326-377.

LILIEN, G. L., A. G. RAO, and S. KALISH (1981) "Bayesian estimation and control of detailing effort in a repeat-purchase diffusion environment." Management Science 27: 493-506.

MAHAJAN, V. and E. MULLER (1982) "Innovative behavior and repeat purchase diffusion models." Proceedings, American Marketing Educators' Conference. Chicago: American Marketing Association, 456-460.

———(1979) "Innovation diffusion and new product growth models in marketing." Journal of Marketing 43: 55-68.

———and R. A. KERIN (1984) "Introduction strategy for new products with positive and negative word-of-mouth." Management Science 30: 1389-1404.

MAHAJAN, V. and R. A. PETERSON (1979) "Integrating time and space in technological substitution models." Technological Forecasting and Social Change 14: 127-146.

———(1978) "Innovation diffusion in a dynamic potential adopter population." Management Science 24: 1589-1597. (See also, Management Science (1982), 28: 1087.)

MAHAJAN, V. and M.E.F. SCHOEMAN (1977) "Generalized model for the time pattern of the diffusion process." IEEE Transactions on Engineering Management EM-24: 12-18.

MAHAJAN, V. and Y. WIND (1985) Innovation Diffusion and New Product Forecasting. Working paper. Dallas: Cox School of Business, Southern Methodist University.

———and S. SHARMA (1983) "An approach to repeat purchase diffusion models." Proceedings, American Marketing Educator's Conference. Chicago: American Marketing Association, 442-446.

MAHAJAN, V., K. E. HAYNES, and K. C. BAL KUMAR (1977) "Modeling the diffusion of public policy innovations among the U.S. states." Socio-Economic Planning Sciences 11: 259-263.

MAKRIDAKIS, S., S. C. WHEELWRIGHT, and V. E. McGEE (1983) Forecasting: Methods and Applications. New York: John Wiley.

MALECKI, E. J. (1977) "Firms and innovation diffusion: examples from banking." Environment and Planning 9: 1291-1305.

MANSFIELD, E. (1961) "Technical change and the rate of imitation." Econometrica 29: 741-766.

MARTINO, J. P. (1983) Technological Forecasting for Decision Making. New York: Elsevier North-Holland.

MATE, K. (1982) Optimal Advertising Strategies for Competing Firms Marketing New Products. Working paper. St. Louis: School of Business, Washington University.

MEADE, N. (1984) "The use of growth curves in forecasting market development—a review and appraisal." Journal of Forecasting 3: 429-451.

MIDGLEY, D. F. (1976) "A simple mathematical theory of innovative behavior." Journal of Consumer Research 3: 31-41.

MONIN, J. P., R. BENAYOUN, and B. SERT (1976) Initiation to the Mathematics of the Processes of Diffusion, Contagion and Propagation. Paris: Mouton.

OLIVER, F. R. (1964) "Methods of Estimating the Logistic Growth Curve." Applied Statistics 13: 57-66.

OLSON, J. A. (1982) "Generalized least squares and maximum likelihood estimation of the logistic function for technology diffusion." Technological Forecasting and Social Change 21: 241-249.

OSTER, S. (1982) "The diffusion of innovation among steel firms: the basic oxygen-furnace." Bell Journal of Economics 13: 45-56.

PERRY, J. L. and K. L. KRAEMER (1978) "Innovation attributes, policy intervention, and the diffusion of computer applications among local governments." Policy Sciences 9: 179-205.

PESSEMIER, E. A. (1977) Product Management: Strategy and Organization. New York: John Wiley.

PETERSON, R. A. and V. MAHAJAN (1978) "Multi-product growth models," pp. 201-231 in J. Sheth (ed.) Research in Marketing. Greenwich, CT: JAI Press.

PIELOU, E. C. (1969) An Introduction to Mathematical Ecology. New York: John Wiley Intersciences.

PITCHER, B. L., R. L. HAMBLIN, and J.L.L. MILLER (1978)a "The diffusion of collective violence." American Sociological Review 43: 23-35.

RANDLES, F. (1983) "On the diffusion of computer terminals in an established engineering environment." Management Science 29: 465-475.

RAO, R. C. and F. M. BASS (1984) Dynamics of New Product Prices: Theory and Evidence. Working paper. Dallas: School of Management, University of Texas.

RAPOPORT, J. (1978) "Diffusion of technological innovation among nonprofit firms: a case study of radioisotopes in U.S. hospitals." Journal of Economics and Business 39: 108-118.

RICHARDS, F. J. (1959) "A flexible growth function for empirical use." Journal of Experimental Botany 10: 290-300.

ROBERTSON, T. S. and Y. WIND (1980) "Organizational psychographics and innovativeness." Journal of Consumer Research 7: 24-31.

ROBINSON, B. and C. LAKHANI (1975) "Dynamic price models for new product planning." Management Science 21 (June): 1113-1122.

ROGERS, E. M. (1983) Diffusion of Innovations. New York: Free Press.

SAHAL, D. (1981) Patterns of Technological Innovation. Reading, MA: Addison-Wesley.

SANATANI, S. (1981) "Market penetration of new products in segmented populations: a system dynamics approach.' ' Technological Forecasting and Social Change 19: 313-329.

SCHMITTLEIN, D. and V. MAHAJAN (1982) "Maximum likelihood estimation for an innovation diffusion model of new product acceptance." Marketing Science 1: 57-78.

SHARIF, M. N. and M. N. ISLAM (1980) "The Weibull distribution as a general model for forecasting technological change." Technological Forecasting and Social Change 18: 247-256.

SHARIF, M. N. and C. KABIR (1976) "A generalized model for forecasting technological substitution." Technological Forecasting and Social Change 8: 353-364.

SHARIF, M. N. and K. RAMANATHAN (1982) "Polynomial innovation diffusion models." Technological Forecasting and Social Change 21: 301-323.

————(1981) "Binomial innovation diffusion models with dynamic potential adopter population." Technological Forecasting and Social Change 20: 63-87.

SOUDER, W. E. and A. QUADDUS (1982) "A decision-modeling approach to forecasting the diffusion of longwall mining technologies." Technological Forecasting and Social Change 21: 1-14.

SRINIVASAN, V. and C. H. MASON (1984) Nonlinear Least Squares Estimation of the Bass Diffusion Model of New Product Acceptance. Working paper. Stanford, CA: Graduate School of Business, Stanford University.

STAPLETON, E. (1976) "The normal distribution as a model of technological substitution." Technological Forecasting and Social Change 8: 325-344.

TAPIERO, C. S. (1983) "Stochastic diffusion models with advertising and word-of-mouth effects." European Journal of Operational Research 12: 348-356.

TEECE, D. J. (1980) "The diffusion of an administrative innovation." Management Science 26: 464-470.

TENG, J. T. and G. L. THOMPSON (1983) "Oligopoly models for optimal advertising when production costs obey a learning curve." Management Science 29: 1087-1101.

TIGERT, D. and B. FARIVAR (1981) "The Bass new product growth model: a sensitivity analysis for a high technology product." Journal of Marketing 45: 81-90.

VON BERTALANFFY, L. (1957) "Quantitative laws in metabolism and growth." The Quarterly Review of Biology 32: 217-231.

WALKER, J. L. (1973) "Comment: problems in research on the diffusion of policy innovations." American Political Science Review 67: 1186-1191.

WARREN, E. H., Jr. (1980) "Solar energy market penetration models: science or number mysticism?" Technological Forecasting and Social Change 16: 105-118.

WEBBER, M. J. (1972) Impact of Uncertainty on Location. Cambridge, MA: M.I.T. Press.

WIND, Y., V. MAHAJAN, and R. C. CARDOZO (1981) New Product Forecasting: Models and Applications. Lexington, MA: D. C. Heath.

*VIJAY MAHAJAN is Herman W. Lay Chair Professor of Marketing, Edwin L.* Cox School of Business, Southern Methodist University, *Dallas, Texas and Senior Research Fellow in the IC² Institute, University of Texas at Austin.* He serves on the editorial review boards of Journal of Marketing, Journal of Marketing Research, Journal of Retailing, *and* Marketing Science. *He has written extensively on product diffusion, marketing strategy, and research.*

*ROBERT A.* PETERSON *is Sam Barshop Professor of Marketing Administration and Charles Hurwitz Fellow in the IC² Institute, the University of Texas at Austin. He serves on several editorial review boards, including the* Journal of Marketing *and the* Journal of Marketing Research. *He is the author of over 100 books and articles dealing with marketing research, consumer behavior, and marketing strategy.*